Stealing Home

Jackie Robinson stealing home.

Stealing Home

AN INTIMATE FAMILY PORTRAIT *by the* DAUGHTER OF JACKIE ROBINSON

SHARON ROBINSON

HarperPerennial

A Division of HarperCollins*Publishers*

A hardcover edition of this book was published in 1996 by HarperCollins Publishers.

STEALING HOME. Copyright © 1996 by Sharon Robinson. Foreword copyright © 1997 by Reverend Jesse L. Jackson. All rights reserved. Printed in the United States of America. No part of this book may be used or reproduced in any manner whatsoever without written permission except in the case of brief quotations embodied in critical articles and reviews. For information address HarperCollins Publishers, Inc., 10 East 53rd Street, New York, NY 10022.

HarperCollins books may be purchased for educational, business, or sales promotional use. For information please write: Special Markets Department, HarperCollins Publishers, Inc., 10 East 53rd Street, New York, NY 10022.

First HarperPerennial edition published 1997.

Designed by Caitlin Daniels

The Library of Congress Cataloging-in-Publication Data

Robinson, Sharon, 1950–
    Stealing home : an intimate family portrait by the daughter of Jackie Robinson / Sharon Robinson; with a foreword by Jesse Jackson.
      p. cm.
   ISBN 0-06-092840-9 (pbk.)
    1. Robinson, Jackie, 1919–1972. 2. Baseball players—United States—Biography. 3. Robinson, Sharon, 1950– . 4. Afro-American families. I. Title.
  [GV865.R6R595 1997]
  796.357'092—dc21
  [B]   97-5868

97 98 99 00 01 ❖/RRD 10 9 8 7 6 5 4 3 2 1

To my strong, sensitive, and very wise son,
Jesse Martin Robinson Simms,
whose presence in my life makes me feel
that everything is possible

CONTENTS

Photographs follow page 150.

ACKNOWLEDGMENTS

A project of this magnitude whose work spans nearly a decade would not have been possible without the assistance, support, and encouragement of my family, friends, and colleagues. I am truly grateful.

To begin with I must thank my dear friend and writer Judy Andrews, who convinced me that my story would help others and then edited an early version of this manuscript. A special thanks to Marie Brown, my agent and friend, for her unfailing belief in the project, advice, patience, and persistence; and to Wendy Wolf, my original editor at HarperCollins, for her honest appraisal, sustained interest, and acquisition of *Stealing Home*. Thanks to Peternelle van Arsdale, who inherited the manuscript from Wendy, asked the hard questions, insisted that I dig deeper, and did a superb job of editing the entire manuscript, and her assistant Kristen Auclair. Thanks to writers Barry Beckham, Herb Boyd, and Pattie Bryan, who helped me to shape the book proposal. A special thanks to editor Tom Bedell, who edited many of the chapters before they were sent to HarperCollins. Thanks to my friends Santita Jackson, Brenda Cooper, Janus Adams, Barry Saunders, Julian Johnson, Veronica Greenwood, Heather Reynolds, Carole Hall, Burt Hoffman, Robin Bell, Daphne Muse, and Lynette Teich; my reader Helen Varney; my attorneys Cathy Frankel and Martin Edelman. In addition to individuals there are several institutions which were particularly supportive: the Jackie Robinson Foundation, the United Negro College Fund, and Yale University School of Nursing.

My thanks to historian Michael Lutzker, who compiled materi-
als for the Jackie Robinson Foundation archival collection. Thanks
to the following individuals for their time and generous sharing of
memories: David Robinson, Marian Logan, Evelyn Cunningham,
Andrea Simon, Jack and Rudy Gordon, Bradley Gordon,
Cleveland Sellers, Candace Allen, Willette Bailey, Dr. Anna B.
Coles, Billie Allen Henderson, Reverend Jesse L. Jackson, Frank
Robinson, Kim Dawson, Issac Parham, and Frank Jerebek.
Gratitude to my wonderfully supportive husband, Molver Fieffe,
and son, Jesse Simms.

And, lastly, my mother, who raised me in her image, shared the
pleasure and the pain, struggled with me to remember moments
we would both rather forget, and rejoiced with me over special
moments that shall remain embedded in our souls. *Stealing Home* is
about home and stolen moments. Our home was centered around
my father but our mother was the core.

FOREWORD

In *Stealing Home,* Jackie Robinson's daughter, Sharon, has afforded us the rare opportunity to enter into the home that Jack built and his wife, Rachel, warmed. Through Sharon's eyes, we see the other side of fame and learn more about Jackie's strengths.

Jackie Robinson was our hero, but we were not there to support him in private. The public never saw Jackie agonize. We saw only the results—the finished product; she witnessed the process—the pain and pleasure. Sharon has allowed us inside. Her memoir, *Stealing Home,* is a metaphor for many aspects of American life.

There is a high failure rate among the children of the successful and famous. They must learn that too much proximity to heat burns you up and too much distance freezes you out. Sharon's journey to self-discovery is inspirational. The fact that she is a professional nurse-midwife, writer, and has also raised a son who is now going to UCLA means that she prepared herself to live beyond her father's memory.

In Greek history, there is something called *Chronos:* the fullness of man's time, the calendar. There is also something called *Kairos:* the fullness of God's promise in history. Whenever Chronos and Kairos come together, some historical moment comes forth with awesome impact. It's unmistakably the presence of God in his fullness that eclipses this special moment. Such was the case with Jackie Robinson. He represented an explosive moment in American history.

It was just after World War II—the world was in turmoil. Fifty-six million people had been killed in the war. Blacks shed blood on the battlefield without the honors that they deserved. Some are just receiving them fifty years later. Many of the big athletic leagues were suspended. Coming after the war there was a revival of American life. Baseball, the American pastime, helped by providing a great escape.

In 1947, the combination of Branch Rickey and Jackie Robinson created a significant breakthrough in bringing down the cotton curtain. These two men represented the meeting of opportunity and preparation. Jackie had the preparation, but so did Josh Gibson and others. Rickey provided the opportunity to act on that preparation.

The years 1947 through 1949 must have been hell. In many of the places the Dodgers played, Jackie could not stay in the same hotel with his white teammates. When stealing home on the baseball field, Jackie had to absorb the balls being thrown at this head. He had to absorb referees calling balls strikes. He had to absorb the pain for the benefit of his country and his race. Jackie Robinson was a baseball player, national conscience, and social transformer all at the same time. When Jackie stole home, he ripped down the cotton curtain.

Jackie Robinson led the movement in the North eight years before Dr. King came on the scene in 1955. What Dr. King did as a preacher, prophet, and freedom fighter was considered hard news by the media and was relegated to the margins of coverage. We know far more about Dr. King in death than we did in his lifetime. Jackie, on the other hand, was at the center of the entertainment media. He was an athlete, entertainer, emancipator, and social transformer. Although Dr. King was periodically heard from a national platform, he always had to struggle, competing with Congress and presidents for hard news coverage. Moments like the speech at the March on Washington were rare. Unlike Dr. King, Jackie had that national platform in baseball every day for ten years and used it to transform the nation.

A moment that stands out in my mind was when I left the March on Washington speech, dashing back to football practice. I saw Jackie and Rachel in the airport. To hear Dr. King and shake the hand of Jackie Robinson in the same afternoon was a providential moment in my life.

Jackie was Sampson who fought the Philistines and won. Like Paul Robeson before him, Jackie was a world-class athlete who used that platform to speak to the broader issues of our time. He did so with a quality of political sophistication that spared him from being isolated as Paul Robeson was. He knew that any time the American press and political forces can marginalize a black leader he loses effectiveness to lead and only succeeds in making whites more hostile to the black cause. Jackie Robinson fought against racism and for the right to win the game by universally accepted rules.

It was a magnificent journey. One could argue that some baseball players could have stolen more bases, gotten more hits, and made more catches, but we don't see any evidence of that. Arguably, no one but Jackie Robinson could have handled the burden with enough dignity.

Today, many athletes who make millions would not make a tax-exempt contribution to a civil rights organization or to a church and work with extraordinary effort to avoid identifying with the heart, soul, and guts of our struggle. They feel it will limit their ability to sell a product or to be elligible for commercials. Jackie, at a time when it was illegal in many states to have a NAACP membership card, would travel the South and give speeches, free of charge, to packed banquet halls. When he challenged a given political issue beyond the scope of baseball, no one ever questioned by what authority he spoke out. That demonstrated an unusual level of maturity and commitment to racial justice.

Jackie was destined to play a pivotal role in American life. From Cairo, Georgia, to Pasadena, California, to breakthroughs in the premiere pastime of American life and on to the 1972 World Series when he made his final public statement to the nation, Jackie Robinson completed a tremendous pilgrimage. From his struggles in the military for first-class stature to his role as a professional baseball player, those forces were to him avenues into his real calling. Jackie's dignity remained nonnegotiable. He had a quality of spirit good for the healing of a nation and generations of unborn.

He was a freedom fighter and an instrument of our people.

It is said that the acorn does not fall far from the tree. Similarly, if there is no tree, the acorn doesn't know which way to grow. It is obvious from reading Sharon's memoir that Jack and Rachel provided that foundation for their children. When the ballplaying was over and the crowds began to hush and diabetes had left Jackie partially blind, Sharon held his hands and literally helped him to see. And now, she has passed that gift of sight and insight on to us through her memoir, *Stealing Home*. For that, we are grateful.

—Reverend Jesse L. Jackson

Stealing Home

In the Shadow of Your Wings

Keep me as the apple of your eye;
hide me in the shadow of your wings.

Psalms 17:8

One of the most historic moments in the twentieth century took place five years before I was born. On August 28, 1945, Jackie Robinson and Branch Rickey shook hands in an office at 215 Montague Street in Brooklyn and nothing in the world was ever quite the same again.

It would be eleven years later, as my father's baseball career was coming to a close, before I would even begin to understand what happened that day. And it was not a particularly pleasant experience for me.

I was six. Mom dropped Jackie and me off at our summer day camps in the suburbs of Connecticut. It was raining, so I ran inside the craft shop to find out my group's assignment for the day.

The assembled campers looked like a sea of white faces. Being the only black girl in a group of eighty campers brought the usual pang of insecurity. The fact that we were all dressed in the same uniform, white cotton short-sleeved shirts with the Camp Hilltop/Camp Holloway emblem on the right pocket, and navy blue shorts similarly embossed, did not make up for the feeling that I was different. But I brightened when I recognized a few friends. I ran to join my group. The room was particularly noisy, full of children, prisoners of the wet weather.

The camp directors came to the front of the room, each wearing a red, short-sleeved knit shirt and khaki trousers. After quieting us, they announced that we would rotate between one of four activities: arts and crafts, movies, games, and lunch. My group was selected for the first showing of films.

As the other campers scattered to their assigned activities, a moan went up from some of the kids in my group who recalled the last film festival we'd sat through: *The 5,000 Fingers of Dr. T.,* and the original *Cinderella.*

We were instructed to sit on the picnic benches that had been brought in from the outside while two counselors set up the portable movie screen in the front of the room and two others adjusted the 16mm film on the projector. As we settled down, the lights were flicked off and the movie began to roll.

The title of the first film couldn't have shocked me more. It was *The Jackie Robinson Story,* starring Jackie Robinson and Ruby Dee. My eyes opened wide, my heart beat faster, and I had to catch my breath as I tried not to gasp. The girl with whom I shared the bench poked me in the ribs.

I sat frozen, listening to the cheers and whistles from the other kids. Jackie Robinson was a hero even at day camp, and they all knew my connection to him. Once he had even visited the camp for a fireside chat with the campers who were staying on an overnight. He had also arranged for sixty of the older campers to attend a game at Ebbets Field between the Dodgers and the Cincinnati Reds.

The film was in black and white. A young actor portrayed Dad in his youth, but as time and the movie progressed, the younger man was replaced by my father. It was Dad's Hollywood debut, and as I sat in amazement on the hard bench, there he stood, tall and statuesque, looking much younger and thinner than I now knew him. But there was no mistaking that broad smile that could light up my world or those strong hands that could practically encircle my waist. He was so handsome. Studying his clean-shaven face on the screen,

I noticed a deep cleft in his chin. The cleft was not so obvious now; his face had become more rounded in his post-baseball days. He smiled again, revealing those perfectly straight, white teeth, which stood out in sharp contrast to his ebony face. I shivered.

Until that day, my familiarity with the movie was pretty much limited to knowledge of its existence. Mom and Dad had told me the history of the film many times, sometimes placing me as much in the starring role as my father. The story went something like this: I was born two weeks before production was scheduled to begin. After my arrival on January 13, 1950 (duly recorded by the New York papers), Dad and Jackie Jr. left Mom and me in our St. Alban's home, while they flew to Los Angeles for the filming. Soon arrangements were made for us to join them on the West Coast. I took my first plane ride at age three weeks. In Los Angeles, Mom, Jackie, and I made daily visits to the movie set. We have pictures of me in the arms of Ruby Dee, who was playing my mother.

If my knowledge of the film was obscure, my understanding of my father's accomplishments was equally fuzzy. By the time I was born the major trauma of the first few years in baseball were behind my parents. I did not grow up hearing horror stories of my father's pioneering efforts. All I knew was that my dad was a famous baseball player on the Brooklyn Dodgers and that people loved to tell stories about his feats. Dad retired from major league baseball when I was six.

Now, I was watching this story about my father for the first time that I could remember in a room filled with white people. I saw a story about his playing, a story of racism and one brave attempt to end an aspect of it. It would have been a peculiar situation for an adult to deal with. It was certainly beyond the powers of comprehension of a six-year-old. As the story unfolded on the screen I saw the school emblems on the uniforms change— from Pasadena City College to UCLA. Then the camera focused on a photograph of my father in an army lieutenant's uniform. Jumping to the post–World War II period, his uniform changed again, to the Negro League's Kansas City Monarchs.

Then came the scene in Branch Rickey's walnut-paneled, smoke-filled office. There was a large blackboard on one wall with the names of players and other personnel in the Dodger organization, down to the lowest minor league teams. On another wall there were four framed pictures: a snapshot of Leo Durocher, the Dodger manager; a portrait of Charles Barrett, one of the all-time top baseball scouts; a photo of General Claire Chennault, leader of the volunteer Flying Tigers, who aided China in its war against Japan; and a portrait of Abraham Lincoln.

"You got a girl, Jackie?" Mr. Rickey asked out of the clear blue.

I stared at the screen and tried to figure out why he wanted to know. I'd heard my father talk to reporters on the phone and knew he could be pretty testy when asked a personal question. I wondered how he would respond.

"Well, the way I've been traveling about the country and not writing as I should, well . . . I don't know," Dad responded after a brief pause. Actually, Dad had been engaged to marry my mother since her freshman year at UCLA, but because of his three years in the Army and the hectic travel schedule with the Kansas City Monarchs, they had been separated for a good portion of the time. Still, they had planned to marry after Mom graduated in the spring and Dad completed the 1945 baseball season. It was on February 10, 1946, that they were finally married, and two weeks later, they traveled to Daytona, Florida, for spring training.

"Is she a fine girl? Does she come from a good family background? Is she an educated girl?" Mr. Rickey asked in rapid succession.

"They don't come any finer, Mr. Rickey," Dad replied, this time without hesitation.

"Then you know doggone well that you have a girl. And you need one. You ought to marry her quick as you can. It will be the best thing in the world for you. When we get through here today, you may want to call her up, because there are times when a man needs a woman by his side."

The actor playing Rickey, Minor Watson, spoke in his evangelistic style. His piercing eyes, hooded by bushy eyebrows, never left my father's equally piercing stare. Rickey offered Dad a seat in one of the overstuffed chairs opposite his desk. They sat and looked at each other for a few moments. Mr. Rickey chewed on his cigar.

"Do you have any idea, Jackie, why we are meeting here today?"
Mr. Rickey asked.

Dad said he only knew what Dodger scout Clyde Sukeforth, also
at the meeting, had told him: "You are starting a new Negro league,
and there will be a team called the Brooklyn Brown Dodgers that
will play at Ebbets Field." But he said this in a voice I wasn't familiar with. It sounded so tentative, so unsure. Dad doesn't speak like
that, I thought. I began to feel increasingly uncomfortable.

"That was what he was supposed to tell you. The truth is that
you are not a candidate for the Brooklyn Brown Dodgers. You
were brought here, Jackie, to play for the Brooklyn organization.
Perhaps in Montreal to start with, and later on . . . if you can make
it . . . the Brooklyn Dodgers."

"Me? Play for Montreal?" He said it in that same quiet, tentative voice. I assumed that he was shocked and nervous.

"I want to win pennants. We need ballplayers. We have scouted
you for weeks. What you can do on the baseball field is a matter of
record. But this is much more than just playing baseball, much
more. What I mean when I say, 'Can you make it?' is do you have
the guts and what it takes to make it?" In the movie, Mr. Rickey
said at this point, "Just relax, boy!"

I nearly jumped up from the bench that I was sitting on. Boy! I
thought. What is this? My brothers were boys. My dad was a man.
Couldn't Mr. Rickey see that? I felt myself get warm, I began to
fidget, I felt even more self-conscious. I hated him talking to my
father as if he were a child and then calling him "boy," especially
in front of my friends. I was well into my adult years before I read
the actual text from their meeting and learned that he had never
called my father boy.

"You think you've got the guts to play the game?" Rickey asked
my father. "They'll shout insults at you. They'll come into you
spikes first. They'll throw at your head."

"Let's say I'm a hotel clerk, Jackie. I look up at you from behind
the desk register. I snarl at you, 'We don't want any niggers sleeping here!' What do you do then?" Mr. Rickey continued before

Dad could respond. "All right, I am playing against you in a cru-
cial game. I smack the ball into the outfield. I'm rounding first, and
I come in to second. It's close. It's a very close play. We untangle
our bodies. I lunge toward you." Mr. Rickey lunged at my dad, his
big fist coming close to his face. "Get out of my way, you black son
of a bitch, you black bastard! What do you do now?"

In the film, finally sounding more like himself, my father said,
"Mr. Rickey, do you want a ballplayer who is afraid to fight back?"
I could tell that his battling spirit was getting worked up.

"I want a ballplayer with guts enough not to fight back,"
responded Mr. Rickey with conviction. And with that, Branch
Rickey Jr. extracted a promise from my father to hold his considerable temper for three years. Rickey was convinced the Great
Experiment would fail if detractors were able to get under my
father's skin and make him blow up in public.

Not fight back? My mind was racing. What did Mr. Rickey
mean?

Watching the film had become almost unbearable. The racial
taunts thrown at my father in the movie were creating some strange
psychological ricochet within me. The movie did not show the next
step in the meeting, but it showed the consequences: my father's first
year in the major leagues, when all of Mr. Rickey's predictions about
harsh treatment and baiting—and worse—came true. But my mor-
tification began to mix with pride. After all, here was my father,
withstanding treatment no human being should have had to put up
with, and doing it with quiet strength and dignity. Here he was,
responding to the challenge with daring skills on the baseball field—
hitting, fielding, stealing bases, and running like the wind.

As the credits rolled and the film went flapping onto the take-
up reel, the lights came back on. It took a few moments for my
eyes to adjust. But it was more than my vision that was dazed, and
that would take years to adjust to. Hundreds of questions for my
parents were generating inside me. I felt ready to burst, or blossom,
and I think I knew even then that something inside me had
changed, and just as my father had changed the larger world, my
own little world would never look quite the same again.

1

The Baseball Years

The urge to question an umpire's eyesight is as
strong in me as the urge to breathe.

Jackie Robinson

My father was a competitor. He more than enjoyed the chance to
compete in a sporting match; he thrived on it, and did so all of his
life. Truly a contest within a contest, his entrance into major league
baseball was his greatest challenge. One contest occurred on the
field and that he was well equipped to handle. Perhaps more difficult though was the challenge of putting his conduct up for constant scrutiny both on and off the field.

I might be forgiven for boasting, but I'm hardly alone in saying
he won both contests convincingly. What has been my lot in life is
figuring out what the value and cost were to my father, mother,
brothers, and to myself. My father had many allies in fostering his
baseball career, but still it was a hard and lonely battle. It brought
him great glory but it forced him to bury some of his basic
instincts. It gave us much; but it required sacrifice.

I doubt that anyone of my family would have wanted the first
black baseball player to have been any other than Jack Roosevelt

Robinson. I know this was true even of my late brother, who suffered periods of great torment as the eldest son and namesake of
his pioneering father. Yet we are never free of wonder, of specula-
tion, about the reasons, timing, coincidence, or fate that, mixed all
together, spelled out my father's name as the first black man's name
written on a major league scorecard in modern history.

Ultimately, it was Dad's strength of character combined with his
extraordinary athletic ability that earned him the opportunity to
write a chapter in history. This athletic genius began to show its
form around the third grade when my father played forward for a
soccer team so good it beat the sixth grade team. Thereafter grade
school kids offered him part of their lunch or money for him to
be on their team. As a teenager, he would band together with other
black kids from Pasadena, and they would head downtown to
Brookside Park to play white teams for ice cream and cake.

At John Muir Technical High School, he won letters in football,
basketball, baseball, and track. At Pasadena City College, he broke
records, including his older brother Mack's broad jump record. My
father was named the Most Valuable Player in Southern California
Junior College baseball. He won the Pacific Coast League conference championship in the broad jump, and a month later captured
the national collegiate broad jump title. At a time when blacks
were not allowed to compete in national tennis tournaments, my
father won the Pacific Coast mixed doubles championship. He
would reach the semifinals in the national Negro Tennis tournament, and win the Pacific Coast intercollegiate golf championship.
He went on to the University of California at Los Angeles on a full
athletic scholarship and became their first four-letter man,
excelling in football, basketball, baseball, and track.

Whenever he competed, attendance escalated. At a Chicago
track meet, a sell-out crowd cheered him on (an additional ten
thousand, mostly black, were turned away). At an All-Star football
game in Chicago, twenty thousand black fans paid to see him play.
Promoters of an exhibition football contest in Hawaii distributed
handbills advertising Jackie Robinson, "the sensational All-
American halfback," as the primary attraction. By 1941, Dad's

senior year at UCLA, he was named football All-American, and was widely acclaimed as the best all-around athlete on the West Coast, if not in the country. He was called cocky and arrogant by some, the man to stop by rival coaches, and "The Dusky Flash," "Midnight Express," and "The Dark Demon" by West Coast sportswriters.

After his discharge from the Army, my father began coaching at Sam Houston College in Houston, Texas. While there, he established the school's first complete physical education training program, installing an exhibit of the many medals and trophies he had won before the war, in the hope that it would inspire the students.

But he wasn't there long. The Kansas City Monarchs had a training site in Houston, and the Negro League baseball team soon enticed Dad to play professional baseball for the lordly salary of four hundred dollars a month. This wasn't bad money in those days. For a period of about thirty years, up until 1947, the Negro Leagues were the most lucrative black enterprise in the country and the stars earned up to a thousand dollars a month.

The transition to the Negro Leagues wasn't easy for the college-educated Robinson, a nondrinker, a nonsmoker, and not about to be a nonentity. He voiced his displeasure with the lack of discipline and professionalism within the league right from the beginning: the long rides on uncomfortable buses, playing in games with little or no sleep, the limited amount of time allotted to training, the cheap motels with dingy and dirty rooms and unusable bathrooms. While the level of play was always extraordinary, the laxity of rules which allowed players to drink and stay out the night before a game clearly affected their performance.

For my father, though, the greatest injustice was the indignity of segregation. His disdain for being relegated to the Jim Crow League only added to his discontent, and though he talked to his teammates about the inevitable end of segregated baseball, many disregarded his words. They had long since given up hope for their participation in major league baseball.

A number of the players felt that even if there was a draft of black players into the majors, Dad wouldn't be selected. As a young

unproven rookie with a fiery disposition, they suspected he would
not survive the pressures of racial pioneering, and couldn't make
the playing grade. Yet there were aspects of his personality and performance that made others sit up and take notice. Monarch manager Buck O'Neil recalled the time the team pulled into an
Oklahoma service station the team had been stopping at for gas for
thirty years. The bus would take a hundred gallons of gas at a time.
But when my father tried to use the bathroom the station manager
said he couldn't.

"Then take the hose out of the tank," said my father.

"What?"

"You heard me, take the hose out of the tank. If we can't use the
bathroom here, then we're not buying your gas."

The manager calculated how long it would take him to make
up the hundred-gallon sale he was about to lose. Then he said,
"Okay, you can use the bathroom. But make it quick."

My father's attitude was fed by the feel of change in the air since
the war. Although over one million men and women served in the
armed services during World War II, they primarily did so in segregated troops. At home, blacks supported the war effort by pur-
chasing bonds, working in riveting shops and in hospitals. In
January 1945, the United States announced that black troops
would be allowed to fight on German soil alongside white troops.
The nearly 250,000 black volunteers were trained and sent into
action on the east side of the Rhine. On April 30, 1945, blacks at
home celebrated the War Department announcement of the success of the effort, and because of the important roles blacks
assumed during World War II, they pressured the United States for
an end to segregation. The success of Jesse Owens in the Olympics
and Joe Louis in boxing added to the pressure that seemed to be
coming from all directions.

In 1945, there wasn't a black player in professional baseball, football, or basketball. However, major league baseball was singled out
as one of the first arenas for change. Sportswriters, leading the
charge, had been fighting to bring down the color barrier since the
turn of the century. By 1945, Damon Runyon, one of the top

sportswriters of the time, was moved to write: "I read a statement in a newspaper the other day that baseball belonged to all the people. This may be true of baseball as a vacant-lot pastime, but it is definitely not true of organized or professional baseball, and it is sheer hypocrisy to say that it does. If baseball belongs to all the people and the people had a vote in its conduct, Negroes would be permitted to play in organized baseball if they could make good by the same standards set for the whites."

Black sportswriters not only led protests against the color line in print, they took action. The *Pittsburgh Courier* waged a "Double-V" campaign, calling for victory at home as well as overseas. Joe Bostic of the *People's Voice* took two players from the Negro Leagues to Bear Mountain and demanded that Branch Rickey give them a tryout. Wendell Smith from the *Pittsburgh Courier* and Billy Rowe, a photographer for the same paper, were instrumental in forcing the issue and smoothing the way for the black players once the color line was broken.

Members of the black press organized an "End Jim Crow in Baseball" committee to pressure major league teams to sign black players. Committee members included the head of the Actor's Guild, Stella Adler, actors Louis Calhern, John Garfield, Sam Jaffe, and Paul Robeson, the lyricist Oscar Hammerstein II; poet Langston Hughes; William O'Dwyer; and Congressman Adam Clayton Powell. At the opening of the 1945 Yankee season the group picketed outside the stadium.

A major roadblock to integrated baseball was Commissioner Judge Kenesaw Mountain Landis, who adamantly refused—at the baseball owners bidding—to consider the question. But Landis died on November 24, 1944, and his successor, A. B. "Happy" Chandler, sang a different tune: "If a black boy can make it in Okinawa and Guadalcanal, hell, he can make it in baseball. . . . I don't believe in barring Negroes from baseball just because they are Negroes."

Meanwhile, Brooklyn Dodger general manager and part owner Branch Rickey was in the process of building a dynasty. The Dodgers, like many other clubs, had lost most of their seasoned players to World War II. Rickey convinced his board of directors to let him sign players of promise regardless of their status within the armed forces, and by 1945, he was determined to find the right black player and sign him to the Brooklyn Dodgers.

Rickey had put considerable thought into the type of individual he needed to fulfill this mission. The candidate did not have to be the best ballplayer, but he needed superior skills. What he really needed was the ability to maintain his competitive peak in spite of pressure and abuse. He needed to exemplify self-control and dignity.

As the scouts sent reports back to Rickey, he reviewed them carefully. Some players were eliminated because of their advancing age, and some were still in the armed services. Others reportedly drank too much or womanized. But by May of 1945, Rickey was pretty much convinced he had his man.

Again, he reviewed the reports from key scouts. George Sisler's report declared unequivocally that Jackie Robinson could run exceptionally well, that he had a slightly better-than-average arm; that he had tremendous possibilities as a hitter. Tom Greenwade called Jackie Robinson the best bunter in baseball. Wid Matthews reported that Jackie Robinson protected the strike zone better than any rookie he had ever seen. Matthews concurred with Sisler that Jackie Robinson was very fast, though he also agreed, much to Branch Rickey's concern, that he might not have a strong arm.

As the Monarch season came to a close, my father had played in forty-one games, hit .345, with ten doubles, four triples, and five home runs, and he was selected to play in the thirteenth annual East-West game (the Negro League equivalent to the All-Star Game) at Comiskey Park in Chicago. The West, with Satchel Paige pitching, had won the championship for two years in a row. The East had such notables as Buck Leonard from the Homestead Grays, first baseman Josh Gibson, and catcher Roy Campanella. Dad, playing alongside the legendary Paige, was the West's shortstop.

Although Robinson's brief stint with the Monarchs had not established him as a star or even "one of the boys," Rickey's confidence grew. He sought the opinion of others who knew the man. One of the men he consulted was Wendell Smith, who gave his unquestioned support. Rickey went to California, where he learned that in addition to Dad's fierce competitive spirit, he was also a man of deep conviction; a fighter when confronted with racism. College-educated, he was articulate and witty. A proud man with a hot temper. A man committed to one woman. A Methodist from a devote Christian home. A man who had served his country in the armed forces and worked his way through college. A man who demanded equality and fought segregation. He learned of my father's court-martial in 1944, while a soldier at Fort Hood, Texas, for refusing to move to the back of a Texas bus. He was ultimately cleared, and honorably discharged from the Army.

While Rickey was satisfied with the information he had gathered, he had one final test. The face-to-face interview. Rickey believed that nonresistance was the only way to break the color barrier, and he needed to know for himself if Jackie Robinson could hold back his aggressiveness in the face of direct attack.

In late August, while the Monarchs were playing the American Giants at Comiskey Park in Chicago, Clyde Sukeforth, the third scout and Rickey's most trusted assistant, was sent out with orders from Branch Rickey: "If you like his arm, bring him in!"

When Sukeforth approached my father at Comiskey Park before the scheduled Monarch's game he found a clearly defensive man. Sukeforth explained that he had been sent by Rickey to observe my father's throwing ability, but Dad had injured his questionable arm landing on his shoulder in a previous game and wasn't scheduled to play. Sukeforth decided to take the chance anyway; he invited Dad to Brooklyn.

My father was skeptical. Like a number of other players in the Negro Leagues, he had been approached by scouts before, pretending to represent the major leagues. And those black ballplayers who had made trips to major league training camps played well and left disappointed. My father was one—he'd had an earlier tryout with the Boston Red Sox arranged by Wendell Smith—and heard nothing.

At a second meeting later that evening in the scout's hotel room, Dad grilled Sukeforth. He wanted to know why Branch Rickey was so interested in seeing him. Dad sensed that it was more than an interest in obtaining a shortstop for the Brown Dodgers. Since Dad was unable to play for a week, the two agreed that the timing was perfect for the meeting. Dad met Clyde Sukeforth the next day in Toledo where he was scouting another player, and they traveled together to the three-hour meeting in Rickey's office at 215 Montague Street in Brooklyn.

The three-year search, which cost the Dodger organization thousands of dollars, was over. On October 23, 1945, the Dodgers announced the signing of Robinson by Montreal, their top farm club. The announcement noted that if Robinson did well, he would be promoted to the Dodgers.

The country reacted with deep feeling to the announcement of Jackie Robinson's signing with Montreal. The supporters outnumbered those opposed to integration of the national pastime. Some questioned Mr. Rickey's motivation; others felt the country was better off with segregation. Executives within baseball who were cautious publicly with their disapproval of Rickey's move, privately condemned his action. African-Americans rejoiced at the news and Wendell Smith observed that "Robinson has the hopes, aspirations and ambitions of thirteen million black Americans heaped upon his broad, sturdy shoulders."

Rickey knew that one of his big problems in introducing a black into baseball was not to convince the public but rather to persuade Dad's future Dodger teammates, many of them from the South. To help smooth the transition, Rickey arranged a seven-game series between the Dodgers and Montreal.

The plan worked in one sense—crowds came to the parks to see firsthand the man creating such a stir and Dad batted a sizzling .625 over the series. But it backfired in another, because some of the Dodger players were antagonized. Three drew up a petition saying they'd rather be traded than play with a black teammate. They convinced few to sign, but when manager Leo Durocher heard about the petition he blew his stack. In *Rickey and Robinson,*

Harvey Frommer wrote that Durocher called a midnight meeting of the entire team and chewed them out: "'I don't give a shit about the way you feel,' he screamed. 'It doesn't mean a thing to me whether the guy is blue or orange or black or if he is striped up like a fucking zebra. I manage this team. I say he plays. I say he can make us all rich. I say that if you can't use the dough I'll see to it that you get the hell out of here.'"

As it turned out, the 1946 Montreal Royals attracted fans in record numbers, and are recorded as one of the greatest teams in the history of minor league baseball. The Canadians loved Jackie Robinson. Black fans flooded to the International League ballparks to see my father play. And within two months, Dad had won over most of his teammates. My father had a remarkable season. He led the league in hitting with a .349 average and in runs scored with 113. He finished second in stolen bases and drove in 66 runs. He also had the highest fielding percentage of the league's second basemen. At the end of the season he was instrumental in helping Montreal win the minor league World Series. Montreal fans surged onto the field toward Dad, who tried to run away, having no idea what the mob had in mind. They lifted him onto their shoulders in joy.

In spite of his tremendous display of talent during the 1946 season, Rickey still had not promoted my father to the majors by the start of the 1947 season. The tension had an adverse effect on Dad's health. He suffered from recurrent stomach problems, which caused him to sit out a number of exhibition games. On April 10, 1947, less than a week before the official opening of the season, in the final exhibition game between the Dodgers and Montreal, before a crowd of fourteen thousand fans, my father got up to bat in the sixth inning and hit into a double play. At the same instant that he hit into the double play, Arthur Mann, Mr. Rickey's assistant, circulated an announcement in the press box. It read: "The Brooklyn Dodgers today purchased the contract of Jack Roosevelt Robinson from the Montreal Royals. He will report immediately." As Dad trotted back to the dugout, his teammates cheered his promotion.

April 15, the Dodgers opened their regular season with a game against the Boston Braves at Ebbets Field. Dad's first two games in Dodger blue were uneventful. Game three was a different story. With thirty-seven thousand fans in attendance at the Polo Grounds, Dad hit his first major league home run. The next day the Dodgers played the New York Giants in the afternoon before a record fifty-two thousand. My father would later write that his biggest thrill in baseball was not that first day, but opening day of the 1947 World Series: "I found myself standing at attention with the other Brooklyn Dodgers in Yankee Stadium, listening to the music of the 'Star-Spangled Banner.' I had finished my first season as the first Negro in major league baseball. . . . But it wasn't until I was standing before the World Series crowd in Yankee Stadium, watching the flag flutter upward in centerfield and hearing the wonderful sounds of our national anthem, that I felt able to say to myself, for the first time, 'Well, you made it.'"

Making it through that first year exacted a heavier toll than any-one realized until many years later. Just as Branch Rickey promised, Dad had to remain silent and grit his teeth against ter-rible taunts and vicious spikings. He received racist letters and threats to his life. Once in Cincinnati some men who dubbed themselves "The Three Travelers" wrote to Dad and told him they would shoot him on the field if he played that afternoon. When he showed the note to the other Dodger players, Gene Hermanski said, "Don't worry, Jackie. We'll all go out there wearing uniforms with 42 on our backs and we'll all black up our faces. Then they won't know which one to aim at." They swept the Reds in a dou-bleheader that day and in the seventh inning of the first game Dad hit a home run. When he crossed the plate, Cal Abrams grabbed him anxiously and said, "Get into the dugout quick before they take a shot at you."

Dad laughed at Cal Abrams's concern and didn't give the Three Travelers a second thought. But that night while Dad was sitting alone in his hotel room, the door opened and three strange men walked in. He wrote in his autobiography that he almost had a heart attack. It turned out that one of the men was a bellboy and the other two were incoming guests. The clerk at the desk had given them his room by mistake, thinking it was vacant.

Despite the occasional camaraderie Dad shared with the other players, he was essentially alone. One columnist wrote that Dad was so isolated from his teammates that he was "the loneliest man ever seen in sports."

Obstacles were put in his pathway at each turn. Once, when the Dodgers got off the train in Philadelphia, taxis were waiting to take them to the Benjamin Franklin Hotel. When they arrived the team was told there were no rooms. The manager added, "And don't bring your team back here while you have any Nigras with you!" The entire team had to move to a different hotel.

Meanwhile, my father received hero worship from the proud black fans. One funny story was told about a black woman listening to an announcer report that Jackie stole a base. "See, I knew they would accuse that boy of something wrong. Just 'cause he's colored. I know Jackie's a fine boy and wouldn't steal anything."

In spite of the three years of holding his emotions in until they nearly boiled over, Jackie Robinson was a star competitor on the baseball diamond. The ballparks were jammed with capacity crowds and all eyes were on Jackie Robinson. The most exciting player on the field, he won over the critics of the experiment. At home, families gathered around the radio. (There was no television coverage.) If there was any doubt, the numbers didn't lie. As the saying goes, you can look it up. In his first year in the majors he batted .297, led the league in stolen bases, the Dodgers in home runs. But it was more than numbers. Dad brought an element of excitement to the game. He danced between bases, choosing the least suspected moment to steal from one base to another. He perfected the art of stealing home, the most daring of baseball moves. He bunted during a time when the art had all but been forgotten. In his first year with the team, my father helped propel the team to the pennant and won the Rookie of the Year Award the first time it was given. Two years later, he led the league in batting (.342) and stolen bases and won the Most Valuable Player Award.

After 1949, Dad went on to have five more great years in baseball, the glory years for the team, which culminated in 1955, the
year the Brooklyn Dodgers won their only World Series. He finished with a lifetime batting average of .311.

To summarize his career in less than a chapter is impossible and
unnecessary given the many other volumes devoted to it. But it's
useful to remember that his career, unlike any other player in history, was always on two tracks. One was devoted to pure accomplishment, the other to the burden of character.

In 1949, Rickey released Jackie from his three-year pledge. The
competitor returned, sometimes in full fury, though not without
warning. "They'd better be prepared to be rough," my father said
of competitors—and umpires—"because I'm going to be rough
with them."

He was and it didn't sit well with many. Dad found that sportswriters and fans who'd regarded him as polite and soft-spoken
thought of him differently when the wraps were off. "I was called
a troublemaker, a swell-headed wise guy, an uppity nigger." Toward
the end of his career he would write about it:

> There are many people who think that a Negro, because he
> is a Negro, should always behave even in the heat of sports
> competition with the subservient humility of a Pullman
> porter. But in my case it goes a little deeper than that. Ever
> since I came up to the Dodgers I have been resented, not just
> because I am a Negro, but because I was the Negro who
> broke the color line in baseball. This theory is not entirely
> mine. It was expressed by many sportswriters. Tom Meany, for
> example, once wrote about me, "When he protests a decision,
> it becomes an issue. When Roy Campanella, Larry Doby of
> the Indians, or Monte Irvin of the Giants [other early black
> players] protests a decision not too much attention is paid to
> it. Robinson is simply paying the price which always accom-
> panies the trail blazer."

But even my father admitted that he went over the line sometimes: "I had too much stored up inside." More than one of his

colleagues have suggested it was the years of holding back which killed my father, not his illness.

As Dad's personality and competitiveness came through, his popularity with the press waned. My father, at the age of thirty-seven, had passed his playing peak. His mentor and friend Branch Rickey had moved on to the Pittsburgh Pirates. And on December 13, 1956, the Brooklyn Dodgers announced that my father had been traded to their arch-rival, the New York Giants, for a left-handed pitcher named Dick Littlefield and a reported thirty thousand dollars.

Unlike today, players then had very little say over their contracts. The team owners and management made the decisions. In my father's case, he had passed his prime and his days in professional sports were numbered. The Dodger management recognized this and they were in search of younger members to move up the ranks. Moving my father into management was not an option at a time when black players were barely accepted and black coaches unheard-of.

When my father learned of the Dodgers plan to trade him, he told the press, "I'll give all I've got." He was just playing it cool though; he had already made another commitment.

The loyal fans exploded. Letters poured into our home and to Dodger headquarters. Some of the envelopes had no more address than: The Great Jackie Robinson. The post office knew where we lived.

"Dear Jackie," they universally began:

"I am a 15 year-old Dodger fan, and like every other Dodger fan I was shocked and utterly disgusted at the news of your being traded to the Giants."

"A disgraceful act and a blow to your many fans," emphatically stated a woman from Ohio.

A seventy-five-year-old man described the Dodger team as having, "Lost its odor and honor."

A woman from New Jersey wrote in the heat of indignation directly to the general manager, Buzzie Bavasi: "You have broken my heart and practically ruined my Christmas by selling Jackie Robinson."

"I lost my breath," another wrote.

Some of the fans offered advice. One who called himself a member of the Faithful Flock made a biblical comparison: "You have to endure great sufferings and abuse to play baseball in the Majors and to show the way for your race, whereas Christ had that cross to carry to Calvary. You both carried your crosses to prove to the world that all men are equal. Owner Walter O'Malley and Buzzie Bavasi, I guess, could be compared in my opinion to Judas Iscariot, who sold our Lord for 30 pieces of silver."

"Go out in glory."

"Thanks for the great thrills you've given me for the past nine or ten years!"

Unknown to the Dodger establishment, the media, or the fans, three days prior to the announcement that he had been traded, Dad had met with the president of Chock Full O'Nuts, William Black. On December 12, he signed a two-year contract with the corporation. He then sold the exclusive rights to his retirement story to *Look* magazine.

My father had moved beyond baseball. And yet he was surprised when the call came in saying that he had been traded. He was tempted to tell Bavasi to go to hell, but he kept to his agreement with *Look* not to release the news of his retirement until after their story broke.

When the January issue of the magazine hit the stands, the baseball world and the media went wild. Dad had outsmarted them by declaring his independence. A sportswriter summed it up. "Robinson's exit from baseball had generated the same type of rhubarb as did his entrance."

For major league baseball my father's retirement signaled the end of an era; for me, it signaled the beginning of our family life.

2

103 Cascade Road

While my dad's baseball career demanded that from February through November he would be on the road, home remained his focal point. He wrote us letters, telephoned twice a day, told us that he missed us, sent Mom flowers, and flew us to Florida for portions of his spring training season. Having grown up economically deprived and without the presence of his father, Dad wanted to do so much more for his children.

My father and mother knew that our home, wherever it was, had to be a safe haven against an often turbulent world. A place where we could escape the insatiable interest of the public and constant scrutiny of the press. Toward this end, Mom and Dad made a hard decision, and in the fall of 1954, my family—my mother, father, two brothers, and I—exchanged our New York address in what was reported by *Ebony* magazine in the late fifties to be the most exclusive Negro residential community in America for an all-white exclusive section of Fairfield County. Leaving

behind the Sugar Hill section of St. Albans, Long Island, our new
address became 103 Cascade Road, Stamford, Connecticut.

In Sugar Hill—less than an hour from Manhattan—our neighbors
had been celebrities like Roy Campanella, Count Basie, Mercer
Ellington, bandleader Earl Bostic, and Ella Fitzgerald. In Stamford,
our neighbors were exclusively white, mostly corporate business-
men; their wives were homemakers.

In the search, my parents learned that my dad's celebrity status
afforded him many benefits, but he was still looked at differently
because of his skin color. Having fought discrimination all their lives,
Mom and Dad were neither surprised nor discouraged when they
encountered the discrimination that permeated the housing market.

The press, hearing of my parents thwarted search, drew attention to their plight. The publicity generated an outpouring of public support. Communities were suddenly eager to show Jack and
Rachel Robinson that they welcomed them into their neighborhoods. Andrea Simon, wife of publishing magnate Dick Simon,
was one of these outraged citizens. After reading in the Stamford
paper that Fairfield County was one of my parents' preferred areas,
she used her power base within the community to leverage support among the local ministers and real estate brokers.

In a relatively short time, my parents were working out the
details on the purchase of a secluded piece of property with the
foundation of a large ranch-style home perched in the middle of
six acres overlooking a pond.

The surrounding property was perfect. With woods on three
sides, it afforded my family privacy, and my brothers and me, who
were six, two, and four, acres of woods to explore. Even the fact
that the house was unfinished was a plus. My mother, who had a
wonderful eye for design, exquisite taste, and the money to purchase the best, insisted on African mahogany wood paneling and
floor-to-ceiling stone fireplaces, tiled the foyer and lower level in
earth-toned marble and her bathroom in turquoise. Her bathtub
was the size of a small swimming pool and it had brass faucets
curved in the shape of arched fish.

The decision to move to Fairfield County was not an effort to distance us from either the rural poverty of our father's birth, or the urban poverty of his childhood, but stemmed more from my parents belief that the country was the best place to raise children, and their increasingly recognized need for privacy. But while the house, grounds, and neighborhood were everything that my parents dreamed of, they still had to contend with their concerns about raising my brothers and me in an all-white community.

It amazes me how little has changed in forty years. The major difference for African-American families today is that we now know that being able to afford an upper-middle-class lifestyle is only the first step. Once there, we vacillate in some strange space between the white culture of our surroundings and the black culture of our roots. Most of us attempt to strike a balance through membership in black social clubs, churches, and community organizations.

Since my parents were social pioneers, they did not have the benefit of others' experiences. Yet they knew the importance of maintaining a strong connection to the black community. My mother went out of her way to find friendships and social opportunities for my brothers and me with other black children. And our father made national affairs our family affair. Over the years the dinner table conversation revolved around politics, entrepreneurial business and banking, the Black Panther party, the NAACP, Dr. King and the Southern Christian Leadership Conference and their nonviolent antisegregation boycotts and mass marches, school desegregation, fire hoses, battles between demonstrators and the police, the right to vote, job discrimination, and Ella Fitzgerald along with homework, getting us kids to the dentist, dance classes, sports, and bed. In short, we were our own sort of normal.

Dad's mission, which began with integrating major league baseball, continued in other arenas after he retired. He made a point of sharing with us his experiences in the civil rights movement. I grew up watching the civil rights struggle on the six o'clock news and having the visuals reinforced by my father's firsthand reports from his trips South. Around the time of our move to Stamford, my father began serving as the national chairman of the NAACP's

Freedom Fund. In that capacity he traveled frequently, speaking on behalf of the organization. His tours took him from Pasadena, California, to Greenville, South Carolina, to Cincinnati, Ohio, and back to New York. When he came home he was usually full of stories. Sometimes they were funny, like the one about Franklin Williams, his traveling companion and NAACP attorney, running out of fund-raising gimmicks and turning to the selling of kisses . . . my father's. Dad laughingly described the scene of ladies coming down the aisle to give money in exchange for the chance to kiss Jackie Robinson.

At other times the stories were painfully serious and very close to our hearts, because the challenge was being led by children no older than we were. Dad was particularly moved by their courage. He described battles in Georgia, Alabama, and Mississippi as children were put on the front line because of the recently passed *Brown v. Board of Education* decision. I was most fascinated by the story of the nine teenagers who were selected to integrate the Little Rock school system.

In the fall of 1957, news of their struggle was all over television. As the situation heated up, the families of the children contacted my father. I still remember the day he heard from the children directly. When he came home that evening, Dad could hardly wait until we were all assembled at the dinner table to launch into his tale. Dad tended to talk more about his volunteer activities within the civil rights movement than he did about his job, making it clear to me early on where his passion lay and the importance he placed on public service.

Aware of the potential that my father's stories would overshadow ours, my mother usually directed the dinner conversation, so that my brothers and I could share something from our day before our father did: a noble intention that didn't always work. On this particular evening for instance, we had barely raised our forks before he began.

"I spoke by phone with some of the children from Little Rock, Arkansas, today. You know, the ones we saw on television last week attempting to enroll in Central High School. Well, you might also remember that they were stopped from going inside by the National Guard." Dad's voice was deep and yet soft as he spoke. He paused momentarily, looking from Jackie to David and me. I put my fork down, remembering the troubling television coverage.

"To make matters worse, a number of parents have been arriving each morning to make sure that the state troopers do their job. A few parents actually went so far as to try to hit the black children."

I was nodding my head, remembering the scene when adults were pushing and shoving right before the television cameras. As a child, this was a hard concept for me to grasp. It was as if the South was another world. I tried to imagine the scene in front of our school in Stamford. I pictured Jackie and me showing up at our all-white elementary school, and instead of going up the stairs and into the stone building, being stopped at the entrance by men in uniform and parents of the children who were to be our classmates and friends. How would I feel?

Without talking down to us, Dad used this opportunity to explain prejudice. Generally, he moved quietly around the house, but it was obvious that this situation had him worked up and he wanted my brothers and me to understand the situation.

"I suppose we all fear the unknown—the strange, the different. The natural fears of parents are made worse by ignorance, and unfortunately they pass them down to their children. In the process, the stories get more and more distorted and eventually become fact in the minds of the storyteller. The sad part for everyone is that prejudice prevents people from sharing talents which could benefit the whole community. The only way racial discrimination can have a hope of being erased is through exposure. The more people understand each other the less they will fear the differences."

"What did you say to the children, Daddy?" I asked, trying to picture their faces.

"Were they boys or girls?" David added.

"How old were they?" Jackie wanted to know.

Dad smiled and continued with the story of his phone conversation. He reminded us that the boys and girls were high school
students. I felt somewhat relieved to know that they were much
older than we were. I wondered how the children could possibly
learn under such tremendous pressure.

I looked questioningly at Jackie, who was ten at the time, trying
to picture him as a teenager going to high school. I figured my
rebellious brother, Jackie Junior, would arrive at school and when
he was told he couldn't go inside, he would drop his books right
in front of the soldiers (because he'd have to do something defiant), turn around, and go to the movies with his friends. I started
to laugh at that image but then the sound of Dad's voice reminded
me that we were discussing something serious. I took another bite
of the baked chicken on my plate and chewed it, quietly listening
to Dad.

"One of the girls I talked to this morning was named Gloria Ray
and another was Minnie Brown. I told the girls that they were doing
a tremendous job that made us swell up with pride. I wanted them
to know that there were people throughout the country supporting
them," Dad went on. "I couldn't believe Minnie's response. She said
that they were following in my footsteps. Can you imagine?"

Dad's voice had faded. I had to strain to hear him. He was staring straight ahead not really focused on any one person, but I
could still see the tears building in his eyes. I watched as he blinked
several times. His expression said more than his words: a sadness
because the children were so young; a pride in their courage and
determination. I am sure that he also felt good playing a role, and
grateful that the school experiences of his own children did not
include such extreme displays of hatred.

I went to bed that night and dreamed of linking arms with
Gloria, Minnie, Thelma, and Melba. We formed an impenetrable
barrier. Our faces conveyed an unstoppable message. The
National Guard offered no resistance. They parted their ranks
and we entered Central High School. As far away as Arkansas
was from Connecticut, I felt a bond with the children in Little
Rock.

A few nights later we learned that President Eisenhower had sent a thousand federal soldiers into Little Rock to escort the children into the school. Gathered with my family in front of the television, I did not need to be told by my mother to straighten my back. The courage of the Little Rock Nine lifted my shoulders.

I felt lucky because I did not have to literally fight to get into my school. However, over the years, I have come to envy the children in the South. They were in a war that had clearly defined parameters, armed with support from the black community and self-esteem heightened by the role they were playing in history.

At four and six, Jackie and I had set out on an unspoken mission of our parents to integrate our schools. Jackie and I went to our assigned public schools. David, who started school a couple of years later, was placed in private school. While the venues differed and the strategies were much less violent, the result was the same isolation. The kids in our respective schools asked us questions like, Why were the palms of our hands and soles of our feet white and the rest of our body brown? Were we dirty? Did we take baths? I remember the embarrassment and the struggle to come up with an answer that would quickly resolve their confusion. In nursery school, David reacted by refusing to take off his shoes and socks for dance class.

While it was true that we did not have to be escorted by armed guards or hear racial taunts from parents and fellow students, the quiet racism we encountered in our early school years was in some ways more destructive in its insidiousness, leaving nagging doubts that shook the core of our self-esteem. Eventually, my brothers and I realized that as the only black children in our neighborhood, schools, and church, we were living in a world where we didn't really fit in.

The impact this fact was having on our sense of ourselves took years to see. We appeared to be healthy, happy children with lots of friends and the freedom to explore and play. And yet we were confused by some of the messages, at times angry and often alienated.

At Hoyt I was shy, quiet, and undemanding. Teachers had no complaints. It is only on reflection that I realize the shyness masked insecurities. I did not like being different.

I was nearsighted and had trouble seeing the blackboard from my desk. The eye doctor prescribed glasses for my nearsightedness, but I refused to wear the pale blue glasses for fear that the kids would make fun of me. So I squinted my way through elementary school.

I hated to be called upon to answer a question or to read a paragraph and rarely did I volunteer to share an opinion. After all, I might be wrong and the kids would really think that I was dumb. Math was the subject that caused me the most grief. I was doubly mortified when it was my turn to stand up in front of the class and recite the multiplication tables. My mind would go blank and I would struggle with anything above the twos.

In fourth grade I made a conscious effort to overcome my fear of speaking in front of my classmates and I selected a class field trip to the Stamford Police Department for the testing ground. My mother was one of the parent chaperones. My mission was doubly important since I also wanted to impress my mother.

We arrived at the police station a little after ten. The police chief welcomed the class of twenty or so and began the tour. He talked a lot but I didn't hear him. I was so focused on formulating a brilliant question that I wasn't listening. My eyes locked on the giant mural that hung twenty feet above my head. The scene in the mural was of Native Americans preparing for some kind of ceremonial dance. They were armed with spears. The police chief said something about the mural being a gift from one of Stamford's leading citizens. He even gave the approximate time frame the painting represented.

As the tour wound down, the police chief wanted to know if we had any questions. I looked around, not wanting to be the first to respond. James's and Alex's hands went up first, then my hand shot up high in the air. I was sure the police chief couldn't miss it. I didn't hear the questions raised by my classmates because I was repeating my question over and over in my mind.

My heart was beating fast. The palms of my hands were sweaty. Finally, it was my turn. My classmates were looking at me. My mother was looking at me . . .

"Are the Indians still alive?" I blurted out, completely innocent of the ridiculousness of the question. My classmates nearly rolled on the floor. My mother looked at the ground. The police chief held back a smile and did his best to respond in a way that would preserve a shred of my dignity. He repeated that the painting depicted a scene from the seventeenth century. It didn't take a mathematician to figure out that if the Native Americans in the picture were still alive they would be hundreds of years old. I could have died right there on the spot.

When my class got back to the school and reviewed the morning's activity, the teacher asked if the class could identify questions that were inappropriate. Several hands went up. My classmates were eager to bring up my folly. Completely humiliated, I retreated back into my shell and was not heard from again for years.

I chose flight, but David's early school experiences brought out the fight in him. He spent his first eight years at New Canaan Country Day School, an exclusive private day school where the boys were required to wear light blue button-down shirts, navy blue blazers, and khaki pants. They played soccer instead of football, took Contemporary Society instead of history, and studied Latin instead of Spanish. It seemed to me that all the kids had blond hair, blue eyes, and very wealthy parents. I thought the whole scene much too homogenized and decided that my public school experience, though flawed, was infinitely better. When my parents offered me the option of going to private school for junior high, I refused, wanting no part of that strange culture.

Not understanding my younger brother or his circumstances, I assumed he was adjusting. I was also convinced that he had become one of "them." It was years before he told me that there were four or five kids in his class who were openly antagonistic, calling him "nigger." My brother stood up to them, challenging his attackers to a fight. For the first few weeks at New Canaan Country Day School, David fought every day at recess. It took a while before he found an ally. Michael Colhoun, a classmate and champion for the underdog, stood up in front of the class and announced that anyone who took on David took him on as well.

For a while David and Michael fought their classmates together. Realizing that they were winning, others joined in.

Michael was from a prominent New Canaan family. His friendship with David defied the social codes of his class and openly challenged existing prejudices in the world that surrounded them. Michael and David started with New Canaan Country Day School and moved on to Michael's private clubs. The clubs had restrictive memberships, and while David was not allowed to become a member, as a guest of the Colhouns he was permitted to join in the activities. David played hockey, skated, rode horses, and even danced with children from families who supported the exclusionary practices.

When the subject of slavery was covered in their Contemporary Society class, David saw another side of Michael. His ancestors were former slave owners from the South, and Mike had been taught to believe that slavery wasn't bad. Even David's persuasiveness did not sway Mike. Hoping to increase his friend's sensitivity, David suggested that they try role playing. Michael agreed. They designed the parameters for their reenactment of slavery.

David was the slave master. He tied Mike up and beat him with tree branches, making Michael do whatever he wanted him to do. Mike played the game by the rules but at the end of the day remained unconvinced. He shrugged his shoulders and insisted that slavery wasn't all that bad.

As elementary school wound down, David wrote a one-sentence poem to sum up his early years at New Canaan Country Day School:

The Tree

It stands there like a soldier not at all at ease
while children play around it in the summer breeze.

3

Jack and Rachel

The world that my father and mother grew up in was very different from that of my brothers and me. Our father's parents, Mallie McGriff and Jerry Robinson, were sharecroppers on a large plantation outside of Cairo, Georgia. When they met in 1903, Mallie was just fourteen years old and they waited to begin their courtship until her parents sanctioned the lengthening of her dresses, signaling that she was mature enough to date. The young couple courted for six years and finally married in 1909.

As newlyweds, Mallie and Jerry moved into a small cabin on Jim Sasser's plantation. It was one of the largest farms in the area and produced a variety of vegetables, raised cows, and grew cotton. After the birth of Frank, Edgar, Mack, and Willa Mae, however, Jerry and Mallie found it increasingly difficult to manage on Jerry's salary of twelve dollars a month. With Mallie's encouragement, Jerry approached his employer and requested permission to half-crop. The new arrangement would allow Jerry to keep half of the

crop for sale or personal use. Not wanting to lose Jerry, Jim Sasser
agreed.

After years of struggle, Mallie and Jerry's income doubled and
afforded them not only the essentials but also extra money for
entertainment. Jerry, feeling like a new man, ventured into the city
of Cairo, where he was exposed to the allure of city life. Mallie was
a country girl with fourteen brothers and sisters, and she wanted
no part of the city. Jerry's wanderings threatened their marriage,
and in this tense atmosphere, Mallie and Jerry conceived a fifth
child. Nine months later, on the evening of January 31, 1919, my
father was born, the only one of Mallie's five children to have been
delivered by a physician.

Six months later, Mallie and Jerry's marriage had reached
another crisis point, and on July 28, Jerry walked off the plantation
saying that he was going to Texas to seek work. He promised to
send for Mallie and the children after he got settled. Instead, Jerry
boarded a train with a married woman he had met in town and
headed to Florida, never to contact the family again.

When Mr. Sasser learned of Jerry's sudden departure, he
stormed to the cabin demanding to know why Mallie hadn't
warned him so that he could have gotten the sheriff to stop Jerry.
At which point Mallie reportedly replied, "The sheriff? Slavery's
over, Mr. Sasser, and that man is free to go where he pleases." That
statement pretty much summed up my grandmother: feisty, determined, courageous, and deeply religious. Jim Sasser's gall snapped
her into dealing with the implications of Jerry's desertion with
strength and dignity.

Mr. Sasser, determined to have the last word, promptly informed
Mallie that she would be held personally responsible for the har-
vest. He added that the half-crop agreement that he had with Jerry
no longer applied. Before Mallie had time to formulate a plan, Jim
Sasser sent word that she would have to move to a smaller more
run-down cabin because another family was moving in. Mallie
promptly marched off the plantation with my father in her arms
and Edgar, Frank, Mack, and Willa Mae at her side.

Leaving the farming community and managing as a single parent was a struggle. The biggest fear wasn't money, however, but the climate of hatred that surrounded them. It was the Red Summer of 1919, as historians have since labeled it, and while the whole country was torn apart by race wars, the South was experiencing an increase in lynchings, black men and women were being burned alive, and the Ku Klux Klan was well organized and gaining political strength.

Mallie, fearing for her children's safety should she remain in the South, began making plans to leave. On May 21, 1920, she boarded the Jim Crow section of the train bound west with her five children, her brother Burton, and other extended family members. Their destination was Pasadena, California.

Mallie's brother Burton had moved to this city of vast economic disparity and racial segregation years earlier. On his return trips home he had boasted of the beauty of Orange Grove Boulevard with its mansions, lush flowering trees, rosebushes, and orange and eucalyptus trees. When Mallie arrived she found that they would be living on the other side of town where poor families crowded together in cold-water flats in segregated neighborhoods.

Accepting that Pasadena was home, Mallie went out in search of work. She quickly found employment in the homes of the wealthy. She would leave home early in the morning, sometimes returning late into the night.

In spite of the long hours, Mallie's income barely fed her family. There were times when the children had only bread and sweetened water for food or had to go to school so hungry that they wore belts tied tightly around their stomachs to suppress the hunger pains. Meat was served only on Sundays. Vegetables were a luxury. Eating leftover food from Mallie's employers was routine.

While Mallie was often out of the home, she maintained high standards and insisted that her children behave impeccably, get good grades, go to Sunday School each week, and take care of each other. The children did as they were expected and also pitched in to help support the family. They built a shoe box and shined shoes, sold hot dogs at sporting events, maintained paper routes, watered neighbors' plants, even bartered their athletic agility for lunch money.

Two years after moving to Pasadena, Mallie had managed to save enough money to purchase a small house in an all-white neighborhood. A light-skinned black woman who had passed for white represented Mallie in the purchase. The owner had no idea that he had actually sold his house to a black family. When the neighbors learned that a black family had moved into 121 Pepper Street, they offered to buy the house back at a higher price. Mallie turned them down, choosing instead to move in and deal with the consequences. The Robinsons were greeted by a cross burning on the front lawn the night they arrived, and ongoing verbal harassment.

Once, Mallie sent her eldest son, Edgar, to go to the corner store for a loaf of bread. He traveled on his roller skates. A neighbor called the police complaining about the noise that the roller skates made on the sidewalk. When Mallie asked the policeman if there was a law against roller skating, the officer backed down and admitted that the real problem was that the neighbor's wife was afraid of colored people.

When my father was eight he got into a battle of words with the white girl from a house across the street. She stood on the sidewalk and called out, "Nigger, nigger, nigger boy." He stood his ground and shouted back, "Nothing but a cracker."

The girl sang: "Soda crackers are good to eat, nigger's only good to beat." The girl's father came outside and started throwing rocks at my father, stopping only after his wife ran out scolding him for behaving like a child.

Several years after Mallie moved to Pepper Street, two of her other sisters and their families moved up from Georgia and found houses in the same neighborhood. Marylou, one of her sisters, ended up living with Mallie after she separated from her husband. Marylou had a daughter named Jessie and when Marylou died suddenly at work, Mallie adopted Jessie without question, adding another mouth to feed to the household.

To survive, Mallie ingrained in her children the concept of the older children caring for their younger siblings. So when Willa

Mae went to kindergarten and Mallie had no one to care for Jackie, she sent him to school with his sister. The teacher sent Willa Mae home with a note saying that Jackie was too young for school. Mallie ignored the note and sent him back the next day. When the teacher continued to object, Mallie took time off from work to personally address the situation. After explaining to the teacher that the only other option was welfare, the teacher agreed to allow Willa Mae to bring Jackie. For the next two years my father played alone in the sandbox just outside of his sister's classroom. During recess he played with the kids, and when it rained, the teacher brought him into the classroom.

From early ages Mallie's children each displayed unusual athletic ability. Edgar was a master on roller skates and the bicycle. He road his bicycle from Pasadena to Santa Monica so fast that he could beat a car. Frank's tall and slim stature made him a natural for track and basketball. Willa Mae excelled in basketball, track, and soccer and was known as a top sprinter. But it was Mack and Jackie whose skill took them beyond the neighborhood and brought them international acclaim.

Mack started by setting records in track and field in junior high, high school, and junior college. He was a tenth of a second off the world record in the hundred-yard dash and once held the world's record in the two-hundred-meter race. His singular moment of glory occurred at the 1936 Olympics when he won a silver medal in the two-hundred-meter race. His accomplishment was overshadowed, however, by Jesse Owens, who won a total of four gold medals and became a national hero.

Mack's traumatic reentry into the United States reminded him of the plight of even the most extraordinary black man. While he was out of the country representing the United States, Mack was fired from his maintenance job with the city of Pasadena. The firing was a reaction to the black community's protest over the city of Pasadena's ruling that they could swim in the city's pools only one day a week. On sweltering summer days, the black kids could only watch, through a fence, as the white children played in the water. This experience led my father to the conclusion that white people actually believed that blacks didn't get as hot as they did. Fed up with the humiliation, the black community staged a protest outside city hall and then took their case to court. They won. The restrictions were removed from city swimming pools. The city manager, however, angered at their victory, turned around and fired every black man who worked for the city. This included Mack.

With his silver medal prominently displayed in his living room, Mack moved from one job to the next, becoming more embittered with each move. He dug ditches, labored on machines, raked asphalt, swept streets, pumped gas, chauffeured comedian Lou Costello, and was a custodian at Warner Brothers' Hollywood movie studio. While Mack's anger at the injustice grew, his baby brother came along and completely upstaged him. The press saw to it that the two brothers spent a lifetime of comparisons. Mack's singular moment of glory remained the highlight of his life.

While certain aspects of my mother's childhood paralleled my father's, they came from distinctly different family structures and economic circumstances. But just as Jackie's mother had done, Mom's parents, Zellee and Charles Isum, ignored the restrictive covenant that forbade the sale of certain houses to blacks, and sent a light-skinned black man to purchase their house on the west side of Los Angeles.

Rachel was born in the back room of that house on 36th Place. She was Zellee and Charles's only girl between two boys, Chuck and Raymond. Her older brother, Chuck, was the product of her mother's first marriage and spent most of his childhood living with Zellee's parents in Nogales, Arizona. Raymond was the baby of the family.

One of their favorite childhood memories was their years of camping at Lake Elsinore in Riverside County in Los Angeles. The lake and campgrounds, owned by a black attorney, attracted black families from all the surrounding communities. The family found camping a welcome release from the rigid regime at home.

The tendency to run a strict, structured home probably stemmed from my grandfather Charles's years in the armed forces.

He was proud of having served his country during World War I and tended to relive his experience through his children. He spent hours training Rachel and Raymond how to handle a gun, march, stay in a straight line, and keep the gun upright.

Ironically, given his passion for the armed forces, his service in the war left him permanently disabled. He was gassed on his last day of active service and developed a chronic heart condition. By the time Rachel was of high school age, her father could no longer work. He retired a young man after working as a bookbinder for twenty-five years with the *Los Angeles Times*.

Charles's forced retirement sent Zellee into the workforce. She was trained to be a caterer by Crystal Marshall in the dining room of the public library and took classes on cake decorating and baking at the farmers' market. When Mrs. Marshall retired, she turned her customers over to Zellee, who then catered dinner parties and luncheons for families in Beverly Hills, Bel Air, and Hollywood.

Rachel, who was five feet five inches tall at age eleven, passed as a much older child. She worked evenings with her mother in the business and Saturdays in the concession stand in the public library. Industrious and independent, my mother loved working and managed to find humor in the catering business.

Once, when Rachel was helping Zellee serve dinner at the home of one of Hollywood's wealthy families, a piece of chicken fell on the shoulder of one of the guests. Barely able to contain her laughter, Rachel made a quick exit back into the kitchen and fell on the floor in hysterics. After the release, she composed herself and returned to the dining room. She removed the piece of chicken without the woman even realizing what had happened.

Soon after her fifteenth birthday, Rachel got a job sewing baby clothes for President Roosevelt's National Youth Administration. When NYA was disbanded, she told the principal at her school a pitiful story about her family's poverty, and landed a job as a typist even though she had minimal typing skills. Her story of her family's financial neediness was so convincing that over the Christmas holidays a group of white ladies showed up at her house with a basket of food. Mom, embarrassed by her deception, had to run

outside to keep the do-gooders from coming into the house and
seeing for themselves that the Isums were not poor.

Rachel's father's health continued to deteriorate during her
high school years. When she graduated from Manual Arts High in
June of 1940, her father was too sick to drive himself to the ceremony, so Raymond was assigned the task. Unfortunately, he forgot to pick his father up. When Rachel got home from the
graduation ceremonies, her father was sitting on the porch crying.
Charles knew that he had missed his opportunity and probably
would not live to see her graduate from college. In the fall of 1940,
my mother entered the University of California at Los Angeles as
a freshman in the school of nursing's five-year baccalaureate program. As he had predicted, my mother's father died during her
freshman year at UCLA.

During her sophomore year Mom witnessed a very disturbing
moment in U.S. history. Over her childhood years, she had
watched her neighborhood slowly change its complexion.
Japanese and black families replaced the white ones. In December
of her sophomore year, with the devastation of the American military base at Pearl Harbor, American sentiment toward the
Japanese living in America turned ugly and irrational. Her Japanese
neighbors were forced to quickly sell their homes before the government shipped them off to internment camps. The pain of seeing her friends carted away in trucks to some unknown fate was
frightening. But Rachel, like most Americans, could do nothing to
stop the forced exile.

The war provided an economic boost to the country and with the
increased workload and the dearth of men to fill the positions, the air-
line industry began hiring women. Lockheed, based in Los Angeles,
hired women as riveters, and my mother was one of those selected.
Mom worked and continued to attend college. Her job was to remain
inside the aluminum-sided planes and work with the men on the
outside. The men would drill rivets into the side of the plane. Mom,
alongside the other women riveters, was responsible for flattening the
rivets so they wouldn't come out. The job required perfect synchro-
nization, forcing the reluctant men to work with the women.

While studying on UCLA's campus, Mom lived at home and commuted to school each day. For black students, campus socializing occurred at Kerck Hoff Hall, and after class, Rachel and her girlfriends, Hope, Joy, and Melanie, hung out in a corner of the hall unofficially reserved for the black students. They were not without motives. The ballplayers, who had jobs cleaning the hall, would pass through and the girls hung around and waited for them. It was here that my mother and father were introduced by a friend of Dad's named Ray Bartlett. There was an immediate attraction and according to Ray my father's passion for athletics paled after meeting my mother.

It wasn't long before Rachel took Jackie home to meet Charles and Zellee. Her father, suspicious and possibly a little jealous, wanted to know why this college senior and campus hero was interested in his daughter. Her mother, on the other hand, reacted quite differently. She loved Jackie from the moment he sat down in her kitchen. He was a clean-cut, well-mannered Christian boy.

By the second semester of Jackie's senior year at UCLA, he had decided to quit school, go to work, and marry Rachel Isum. As they announced their engagement, Jack and Rachel assured Zellee that the marriage would not occur until after Rachel finished UCLA's five-year nursing program.

My father began the process of seeking work. But instead of finding a job, he was drafted into the Army as a second lieutenant. Because of an old football injury, Dad didn't see combat in Europe but instead battled racism and segregation in the armed forces. He was discharged just as Rachel graduated from college. Rachel then told Jack that she needed some time to explore the world of work before getting married. Family and friends, fearful that Jack would give up waiting, warned Rachel about the lure of independence.

Following her own instincts, my mother spent the summer working in a local hospital, and then traveled by train to New York. Jack took a job as an athletic counselor at a youth camp, then went on to be a basketball coach at Sam Houston College before being asked to play professional baseball for the Kansas City Monarchs. On February 10, 1946, just before spring training, my parents formalized their lifelong partnership in a wedding ceremony at a church in Los Angeles.

Mom and Dad planned on three children. My mother wanted to repeat her family composition with two boys and a girl, and typical of my mother, she did just as she planned. We started arriving nine months after their wedding. Jackie was born November 18, 1946, I was born January 13, 1950, and David arrived on May 14, 1952.

Having survived ten successful yet stressful years of baseball, my parents felt prepared for anything. Parenting, as it would turn out, was by far their biggest challenge. Yet it didn't start out that way.

4

Extra Innings

I've been with some tough guys in my lifetime . . . and yet I say
that if I had to go down a dark alley with one guy, if I had to
make a choice, that man's name was Jackie Robinson.

Irving Rudd, *Bums*

As I remember it, the winter of 1958 was particularly cold, even
for Connecticut. I awoke at my usual time one morning, and
looked out of my bedroom window at a promising winter whiteness. Although the snow had lessened to flurries, I was hoping
school would be closed for the third day in a row.

I wrapped the pink wool blend blanket and the bedspread
around me and began making plans for the day. The worst option
included seven hours of school. But whatever happened, my best
friend, Christy Joyce, would be involved.

My room was quite a ways from the kitchen, but Dad played the
radio so loudly in the mornings I could hear the rhythm of the
1010 WINS announcer's voice, even if I couldn't make out his
words. If school was closed I could stay under the covers long
enough for the house to warm up. Lying perfectly still, I strained
to make out the reporter's words, but I couldn't. Unable to bear
the suspense, I emerged from my cocoon, tied my pink terry

bathrobe tightly around me, and headed toward the aroma of sim-
mering grits and bacon, and the pronouncement of the school verdict.

Dad was at the stove in his turquoise floor-length terry
bathrobe, his back to the marble countertop adjacent to the stove.
He stirred the grits with a large wooden spoon. Mom stood next
to him in slacks and wool sweater, frying the dozen or so slices of
bacon in a large stainless-steel pan. He wasn't dressed for work. A
good sign.

"Is there school today?" I asked, trying not to sound too eager.

"Good morning," Mom and Dad spoke in unison.

I got the message: "Good morning," I replied.

"School will be closed again today," Mom responded. "Even
your father can't get to work. Let's hope the snowplows find their
way to Cascade Road soon, but, until then, we'll just enjoy the
time at home. Go and sit by the fire and I'll bring you a cup of hot
cocoa."

Content with the news that school was closed, I sank into the
overstuffed leather chair next to the stone fireplace, my long slender legs slung over one arm, my head resting on the other. Since
my brothers were still asleep the house was relatively still. I looked
out the picture windows, where the second-story wooden deck
was heaped with ten inches of snow. Icicles hanging off the roof
looked like natural sculptures of gymnasts suspended from parallel
bars, arms linked, each appendage unique in its beauty, yet collectively striking and poised. A part of me wanted to capture and preserve the beauty; another part wanted to share its temporary
magnificence. Sipping my hot cocoa, I tried to figure out how.

Struck with an idea, I slung my legs around, jumped up from the
chair.

"Mom, is it too early to call Christy?"

Mom poked her head in from the kitchen. "Sharon, how many
times have I told you not to yell from one room to the other?" she
scolded gently. Voices were rarely raised in our house. "Wait until
eight o'clock to call Christy. Wake your brothers. Breakfast is
ready."

I was disappointed that I'd have to wait half an hour. Christy and I had been inseparable from kindergarten through junior high; she lived about an eighth of a mile up the road from us, part of a family I considered the archetypical white family of the fifties. Mr. Joyce worked downtown for an insurance company. Mrs. Joyce, like my mother, was a homemaker.

Christy and I shared a passion for dolls, musicals, and water ballets and would happily fill in when our brothers needed a team for football or baseball on the front lawn. We slept over at one another's houses almost every weekend, met at the bus stop each morning, and giggled about the day's possibilities all the way to school. We kept pace with each other, determined to earn the same number of badges as we moved from Brownies to Girl Scouts or remained "in synch" during our annual water ballet performance before our families.

Since we lived in a neighborhood where the boys outnumbered the girls, our parents seemed to delight in our friendship as much as we did. They never failed to mention our good fortune in finding each other. It didn't matter that Christy's eyes were blue and mine brown, that her skin was vanilla and mine chocolate, or that she had straight blond hair while mine was curly and black. We were best friends.

At nine years of age, there were few things that Christy and I didn't share. So when I finally called her that snowy morning, she didn't say my idea was dumb or hesitate to join in my enthusiasm. We agreed that Christy would come over at ten so that we could select the most unusual icicles, break them off the roof, set up a stand at the end of the driveway, and sell them to our neighbors.

Christy arrived later that morning with her two brothers in tow. Danny and Willie headed off to play with Jackie and David, and Christy and I went to work. Mom took our mission seriously; she gave us a card table and material for signs. We set up for business and waited patiently for our first customer. The roads had been plowed and an occasional car passed by but didn't stop. Just as Christy and I had taken to doing jumping jacks to keep warm, my next-door neighbor pulled up and purchased not one but two of our iced beauties. We collected ten cents. It was a modest financial take, but we declared ourselves successful, closed the business, grabbed our toboggans, and raced our brothers down the hill.

After lunch, all six of us descended on my dad. We begged him to let us go skating. It was his official job to test the ice on the lake to determine its safety. It involved an elaborate ceremony, but we always took great delight when he announced that the ice was, indeed, safe.

But before this could happen we had to get him out of the house, no easy feat. David and I scrambled to help him find his gloves, hat, and coat. Then we sat impatiently waiting for him to put on his oversized black rubber boots. The wait was torture. When Dad was properly dressed for the frigid weather, he led the way carrying his equipment—a shovel and broomstick. We followed him through the living room, out of the sliding glass doors, down the back stairs, and down the hill.

As we reached the edge of the lake, Dad proclaimed to the troops hot on his heels, "That's as far as you go." Jackie, David, Danny, Willie, Christy, and I came to an abrupt halt. We lined up along the shoreline, and shouted words of encouragement as Dad proceeded out onto the snow-covered ice.

The lake, which ran the length of our property and then continued for about an eighth of a mile down the road, was a source of great pleasure. In spring we collected polliwogs from its banks. In summer we swam, fished, and rowed the boat to the shallow sandbanks and captured sunbathing turtles. In winter, the lake was reserved for figure skating and ice hockey.

Dad cleared the snow from his path with each measured step. Before he placed one big foot in front of the other, he would tap the ice with his broomstick. From the cleared spot he was able to estimate the depth of the layer of ice beneath his body. After what seemed like forever, Dad would reach the deepest part of the lake, give one last tap with his stick, then turn to us and call out: "Go get your skates!"

We would cheer as loudly as we could and race back up the hill to get our skates and shovels, since clearing the snow off the ice was a big part of the production. But it wouldn't be long before the boys' hockey sticks were battling the black rubber puck, while Christy and I were forming figure eights at the other end of the lake, and Dad had made his way back to the house.

But sometimes Dad's tapping would cause an air bubble to become dislodged. Then a loud rumble would roll across the lake and we would cry out in near hysterics for fear that the lake would open up and swallow Dad. Of course, it never did. But, given the remote possibility, I thought Dad was very brave.

Now I think it even more. He was as brave then as when he entered baseball, a feat it took me years to appreciate. It dawned on me only gradually what it had meant for him to break the baseball color line, the courage it took for him to enter uncharted, and dangerous, waters.

No one really knew what would happen. He had to feel his way along an uncleared path like a blind man tapping for clues. That was Jackie Robinson. And that was my dad—big, heavy, out there alone on the lake, tapping his way along so the ice would be safe for us.

And he couldn't swim.

The first ten years of my life were blissfully uncomplicated. In some ways they bordered on being fanciful, surreal, idyllic.

Dad was a basic kind of guy. Meat and potatoes for dinner, grits and scrambled eggs every morning, a warm comfortable home, privacy, his family, golf, and television. He exchanged cars every two years, yet each one looked exactly like the earlier model. It always amused me when he would go into a restaurant and pretend to study the menu when he would undoubtedly order the same thing—steak and potatoes, veal parmigiana, or fried chicken. Whenever possible, he shopped in the garment district in New York City, to avoid the retail markup in the department stores. He did not drink alcohol, smoke cigarettes, or go to parties. His only vice was an attraction to the horse races. Dad worked hard and traveled often, but as long as we had our mother at home, life remained stable. When Dad wasn't traveling, we could count on

him being home by six. We all ate together in the dining room and
after dinner he was always present in the living room. Dad was very
proud of his family and considered himself a lucky man.

We were an enviable family living the American Dream. Our
perfection was immortalized on the front covers of magazines,
through the television media, and in newsprint. Everywhere we
went people stared, whispered, pointed, smiled, admired us from
afar. Sometimes they came close to ask a question, request an autograph, or share a baseball memory. Even long after Dad retired
from baseball, when we were with him there was no escaping the
fans. Our mother, like our father, was a symbol of perfection—
beautiful, gracious, available, and attentive as wife and mother. I
never questioned her contentment in the role of full-time mother
and wife. I knew that her mother had raised her to believe that a
career was reserved for emergencies and that my father, who had
grown up with the pain of watching his mother work too hard,
wanted his wife to have a different life. Which she did. Mom studied interior decorating, went to classes on flower arranging and
architectural design, and took piano lessons at Steinway Hall in
New York from Juliet Mirova, the concert pianist. She also traveled
with my father and attended functions in his honor. It was our
mother who rose early to turn up the heat in the winter so that
our chilly rooms would be more comfortable when we got up to
dress for school, made most of the decisions about our daily life,
and took us to the doctor, dentist, and Scout meetings. She saw to
it that I studied piano, violin, and ballet; she went alone to PTA
meetings, teacher conferences, and school plays. She got us up on
Saturday mornings to help her and Dad with the yard work. Dad
was so accustomed to Mom making all decisions about us that
even when we asked him if we could do something or go over to
a friend's house his standard reply was "Go ask your mother." It
wasn't that Dad was unconcerned. Rather it was that Mom was in
charge.

Holidays, our extended family gathered at our house in
Stamford. At Thanksgiving, my mother's brother and sister-in-law,
Chuck and Brenda Williams, and their children Chuckie, Kirk, and

Rhoda, Dad's childhood friends, Jack and Rudy Gordon and their son, Bradley, and the Logans, Marian and Arthur and their son, Chip, shared our traditional dinner. The women cooked and cheered the men during their annual father-son football game on the front lawn and washed dishes while the men lounged in the family room watching football on television. At Christmas we cut down an evergreen tree from our yard, helped Dad put the lights on the trees in front of the house, received far too many gifts, gorged ourselves on a pancake breakfast prepared by our father, and had lazy days by the fireplace.

The other aspect of our childhood was regular family vacations. Since even Dad's vacation requirements were quite simple—an eighteen-hole golf course and decent tennis facilities—any resort could satisfy the whole family. Sometimes, Mom and Dad would take us to a Caribbean island for a week of sun and beach play, but one of our favorite spots was Grossinger's, a resort nestled in the Catskill Mountains. It had the added bonus of being available to us at any time for virtually no cost. We had an open invitation from the owner, Jennie Grossinger. So, several times a year, Dad would pack us into his car and we'd head for that region, famous for its green hills, shimmering lakes, kosher food, and nonstop entertainment.

While at Grossinger's, my brothers and I fine-tuned our inherited athletic abilities. During the summer months, I concentrated on perfecting my swimming, stopping to join in the daily poolside calisthenics led by the Grossinger's social director. The butterfly stroke was the only one to defeat me—it required such tremendous upper-body strength. I couldn't seem to get my arms completely out of the water. I finally gave in and settled for comfortably gliding across the pool doing the breaststroke. In the winter months, while David concentrated on perfecting his ice hockey skills, I worked on the more graceful art of figure skating. I practiced, over and over, the spins that sent my short, black-velvet skating skirt twirling about my body.

During the winter months, when golf and tennis were out of the question, Mom and Dad would join Jackie, David, and me for skiing lessons. Dad looked so funny trying to retrain his feet from their natural, pigeon-toed position into the straight line necessary to ski down the hill. We'd laugh at his attempts, but really we were delighted to have the whole family on the slopes.

At its peak, Grossinger's attracted the biggest names in show business, and a host of celebrities and politicians flocked to the region to see and be seen. All this helped to make the nighttime at Grossinger's very glamorous. Getting ready for dinner was always a big production. Mom, with deliberate attention, saw to it that my brothers and I were dressed to perfection. As my family entered the grand ballroom, a hushed silence would travel through the room. The mostly Jewish guests stopped eating, talking, or whatever they were doing to acknowledge our arrival. As we were escorted to our table, which was strategically placed in the center of the room, Dad would stop to shake the outstretched hands.

My mother was clearly the most beautiful woman in the room; my dad, the most celebrated man. My brothers and I, immaculate, polite, and well trained. It was in this very dining room that we practiced our best table manners under the watchful, loving eye of our mother and the two hundred or so guests in the room.

As a child, I was close to both of my parents. From what I remember and have been told, I was an expressive, responsive little girl, easy to please and always obedient. My parents were lovingly attentive but not overly affectionate. In fact, Mom tells me of the time when Dad was innocently rubbing lotion on my ashy legs and I squealed with delight, alerting my father to the fact that his touch was pleasurable. It took years for my father to become comfortable again with physical closeness, so for years, he expressed his love for me in sweet tones, sugary words, hugs and kisses on the cheek. I never doubted for a minute his love or my special place in his life. Take our special father-daughter excursions to New York City. Dad started taking me on daylong outings when I was in grade school and continued to do so throughout my college years. The activities varied as I grew older but the sentiment attached to them was the same. But I would not be totally happy until Dad and I had left everyone behind and were alone in our adventure.

Before we could get to that point there were several steps to our ritual, the first being Dad's approach. He would bend to my level with a twinkle in his brown eyes and ask:

"Sher, want to come to 'the city' with me tomorrow?"

"Yes, Daddy." I would giggle, hug him mightily, and run to share my good news with my brothers.

"Big deal," Jackie would say in his most sarcastic tone, leaving me cold with his chilly expression. I didn't understand it then. I do now. While David and I remember spending special times with our father, I am not sure that Jackie would have had the same recollection. Jackie Junior was born the same year Dad put on Dodger blue for the first time, and his younger years were also the baseball years when Dad didn't have the time to be as indulgent, and private moments were hard to find. Consequently, the two were competitors from the start and never had the luxury of time to develop a friendship. I am certain now that the sarcasm I heard in my brother's voice when we were kids was justified jealousy.

David and I have very different memories. David and Dad could go off on a day of fishing and come back happy and relaxed; Jackie and Dad seemed to always be at odds. Once Dad took David on a drive all the way to Canada just to fish. I couldn't imagine Jackie and Dad spending hours alone in a car. By the time David was ten, he was caddying for our father at the Hubbard Heights golf club. By twelve, he was allowed to drive the golf cart.

After Jackie's rejection, I did not bother to take my news to my younger brother. Instead, I ran down the marble stairs to tell Willette Bailey. I would find her in the wing of the house that she called her home away from home.

Willette was the sister of Florence Covington, whose husband was Lacy Covington, pastor of Nazarene Baptist Church in Brooklyn's Bedford-Stuyvesant section. The Covingtons opened their home to Mom and Dad their first season with the Dodgers. It became a tradition that my family and theirs would have Sunday dinner together whenever the Dodgers were in town. Over the years a lasting family bond was established.

Willette came to live with us when David was born. She offered to help for a few weeks while Mom recovered from a postpartum kidney infection. Those two weeks turned into fifteen years. While for all practical purposes she lived with us during her entire stay, Willette always maintained her apartment on 140th and Edgecombe Avenue in Harlem.

Tiny, with brown skin and high cheekbones, which she proudly pointed out were part of her Native American heritage, Willette was more like a big sister or surrogate mother than a caretaker. Willette and I chatted easily about a range of topics as I helped her set the table for dinner. After the dishes were done, we'd disappear to watch television in the family room where we spooned vanilla ice cream from tall glasses of chilled grape juice and ice cream.

Willette was little but feisty, opinionated, and always took our side even when it came to my parents. As childhood grumbles turned into teenage discontent, Willette stayed close. I'd complain about having been wronged in some way by my mother and she would grumble right along with me. I could also count on Willette to share my excitement.

"Willette," I yelled from the base of the stairs. I hoped she wasn't asleep.

"You don't have to yell. I'm in my room, Sharon."

Feeling sheepish, I wandered into her bedroom. "Sorry. But, Willette, I'm going to New York with Daddy tomorrow . . ."

". . . And you want to pick out your clothes." She had a habit of finishing my sentences. "Okay, let's go upstairs into that messy closet of yours."

As the middle child and only daughter, I held a unique place in the family. My closet, crammed with dresses, skirts, blouses, pants, coats, and shoes, was a glaring testament to my status. Willette and I entered my room in search of an outfit for my trip. My eyes widened as I braced myself for her reaction to the clutter.

"How many times have I told you not to throw your dirty clothes on the floor?" She bent to pick up the pile of blouses and sweaters that blocked our passage. I reached for my baby doll sitting on top of the heap, and put her into her own floral, print-covered cradle.

"I want to wear this!" I spotted one of my party dresses—a yellow organdy that required a full petticoat to give the skirt the swish that it demanded.

"You're not going to a party. You're going to your daddy's office." Willette shook her head disgustedly.

Dad's involvement with the corporate world forced him from his casual elegant look of knit shirts, sports jacket, and pleated trousers into dark blue, gray, or tweed suits which he complemented with fabulous ties. Willette and I had an image to work toward. We had to select an outfit for the occasion carefully. Oh, we had so many choices. But we were nevertheless directed by what we knew Mother would insist on. She would want me dressed up completely, with white gloves, Sunday School hat, and tiny pocketbook. When the weather turned colder, I replaced the white gloves and hat with a white fake-fur muffler hanging around my neck. I had matching earmuffs as well. Perfection was our goal.

The next day, my stomach flipping with excitement, Dad and I were off, challenging the curves of the Merritt Parkway. Driving at least ten miles per hour above the speed limit, he maneuvered the car masterfully, darting suddenly into the left lane to pass the car in front, accelerating into the curve and then switching to the right and speeding straight ahead. I felt as if we were culprits, hand in hand, stealthily dashing from second base to third while the pitcher was still in his windup.

Usually he moved in and out of lanes or sped ahead so smoothly that I was never thrown off balance. But there was a stretch of incline as we crossed into Westchester County that he loved to take barreling upward to its precipice so that my back was cemented to the seat and I would find my eyes staring at the car's gray felt roof. The car would then hit a bump that sent my stomach up to my chest and back down again. We could have been on a roller coaster. I squealed. Dad laughed. No matter how many times we hit that spot, I always had the same surprised reaction.

Gradually, the blurred line of trees along the highway disappeared. The noise level increased suddenly, swallowing up our ears in a roar of disjointed sounds, alerting us that we were entering

Manhattan. I knew that we would be in the heart of the city within minutes. My own heart was thundering. I couldn't sit still. I moved closer to my dad.

Soon he was pulling the car into the parking garage near the Chock Full O'Nuts headquarters at 425 Lexington Avenue and we were being greeted by the attendant. "Good morning, Jackie. What time can we expect you today?" He wrote on the parking ticket and nodded to me.

"About three-thirty." Dad helped me out of the car and held tightly to my hand.

Chock Full O'Nuts was our first stop. We entered the building through the coffee shop on the first level. Dad stopped to greet the ladies—most of whom were black—behind the counter. They always made a big fuss over me, and I would be totally delighted by their questions, their smiles, their hugs. Given this warm reception and the aroma of the coffee and doughnuts, I was perfectly content to stay with the staff while Dad went about his business.

While I was perched on one of the revolving bar stools enjoying a long, rectangular pecan brownie and hot cocoa, the ladies kept me entertained. They loved to reminisce about Dad's years with the Brooklyn Dodgers. Their eyes sparkled, bodies became animated, fingers snapped, and they pointed at each other as they told their stories.

"We'd pack a lunch and go right from church . . . still in our Sunday School clothes," one of the ladies said.

"Once my father and I took the train all the way to Pittsburgh just to see Jackie play. You know that no one since Babe Ruth brought more people into the ballparks," a customer chimed in.

"Do you remember how he kept those pitchers guessing while he danced on and off the base? Then, just when the pitcher figured out his rhythm, he'd steal another base."

"When we couldn't go to the ballpark, we'd crowd around the radio in the kitchen," another lady remembered.

I'd sit entranced by their memories, conjuring up images of my own. Although Dad felt comfortable leaving me with these ladies, he wouldn't be gone for long. My father knew that I would get restless after twenty minutes. Besides, he understood that this was our special day and that I was eager to proceed.

When he returned, it was with a big smile and a quick twist of my stool—a gesture which sent me into a fit of laughter. Then he lifted me off the stool. He took my hand and we said our good-byes once again that day.

Now on Lexington Avenue, Dad hailed a taxi and directed him to take us to 1333 Broadway to the garment district, where Mr. Love's store was located. Dad had met Joseph Love at the ball-park. A week later, the first of a number of large brown boxes arrived at our house filled with dresses for me. A Polish immi-grant, Joseph Love had started his company in 1920 with funds from his army bonus. His timing had been impeccable, for women were entering the labor force and demanding ready-made clothing for their children. Prior to 1919, it had been con-sidered almost a sin to purchase store-bought clothing for children. Love believed that not only should little girls own store-bought dresses, but also that these dresses should be fancy and in pastel colors.

As Dad and I entered Mr. Love's shop, I heard a chorus of voices and then braced myself for the band of salespeople rush-ing to greet us.

While my dad and Mr. Love talked baseball and politics, I was escorted around the shop and permitted to pick out any dress that I wanted, living a child's fantasy of being turned loose in a toy store. I usually managed to select five or six lovely dresses. I still remember some of my favorites: a periwinkle blue dress with a white collar and dirndl skirt, a pink polka-dot dress with match-ing shorts, a gray-check dress with a red petticoat, and a plaid dress with smocking on the bodice done in red, yellow, and green. Before we departed, Mr. Love would promise to send me a box of dresses when his new line arrived. He kept to his word, and for years my closet was filled with dresses that bore his label. I was well into my teens, looking back over our trips to the garment district, before I realized how privileged I had been. All I knew was that I loved the special attention.

The visit to Joseph Love, Inc., was for me. Our second call of the morning was for my mother. It was to one of the lingerie houses in the area. Once Dad and I were seated comfortably, the salespeople would bring out one coat rack after another, each filled with beautiful negligees. I was mesmerized by the romantic negligees and the image of my father buying a dozen for my mother.

"Sharon." It was my dad's voice. I guess my mind had been wandering. "Which one do you like?"

"The peach one," I replied without hesitating, pointing to a long peach negligee with an ivory lace bodice. I could just imagine my mother in that gown. The color would soften perfectly next to her light brown skin.

I had the most difficult time understanding why my mother was so much lighter than my brothers and me. I asked her often, and she usually responded with something about the fact that black people come in all kinds of different shades of skin tones. In the 1950s, the American standard of beauty was gauged by white norms, so I concluded that since she was lighter, her color was better. Trying to get some clarity, I'd persist.

"And why are the underside of my arms lighter than the top?" Mom didn't really have a good answer to that question.

One day Jackie and I cornered Mom in the library. There we were, surrounded by the Encyclopedia Britannica and hundreds of other reference books and histories that might have told us the truth about the mixed blood of African-Americans, asking our mother if she were really a white lady. And, more important, if Mom was white, what were we?

"You're a combination of your father and me," Mom said, trying to reassure us. We finally gave in and accepted her explanations of the varying degrees of chocolate skin.

I was thinking that the light coffee color of her face and arms would look so mellow next to that peach silk negligee with the ivory lace bodice. Now, if it had been for me, I would have picked the pale blue one, because blue was my favorite color.

Dad must have seen my eyes fixated on the blue gown because

he picked that one next. And together we decided on the cream negligee. I sure thought my mom was lucky.

The next thing I knew, my mind was off again. I had such a hard time staying focused and controlling my mental journeys. They just happened. I'm not sure how I went from the lingerie shop to thinking about the doll baby I got the Christmas before.

Mom had said the doll baby was from Santa, but I was suspicious. She was the first thing I saw when I came into the living room Christmas morning. I looked in astonishment at her alabaster skin, blond curly hair, blue eyes, and peachy cheeks. My precious baby lay in a white-skirted cradle. Tiny pink roses cascaded down the sides and eyelet lace adorned the base of the skirt. Only my mom could have selected something so lovely and feminine.

The only black doll that I remember having as a child was made of hard plastic. She wouldn't even bend. But this white baby was soft, flexible, and thoroughly lovable. It didn't matter that the baby doll didn't do anything on her own. She couldn't cry, drink from a bottle, or sing, like the baby dolls of the future, but she was mine. I could give her a voice, and then respond to her needs. It was almost as good as having a baby sister.

Dad's voice pierced through to my consciousness, bringing me back to the moment. Mom's package was ready and Dad and I were off again, hand in hand, each with a box to carry in our free hand. Famished, we planned for lunch, our next and last stop in New York City. We stopped at a restaurant for a hamburger. By four o'clock, Dad had the car heading north, promising to have me home in forty-five minutes.

I'd be too excited to talk or to notice the speed with which we traveled. I couldn't wait to get home and see my mother's expression as she opened the boxes. If my suspicions were correct, Mom's throat would emit those special, happy sounds signaling that Dad and I had chosen well.

I also couldn't wait to get home so that I could change my clothes. Dressing up and going to the big city was exciting and romantic, but I still preferred the freedom of the country, and the comfort of my pants and sneakers. I sighed as we reached the toll plaza that alerted us that we were near the Connecticut border. Our special time together had come to an end. I was my father's princess; he was my hero. And, most important, for those few moments I had him all to myself.

5

Boys and Friendship

Life in the fifth grade took on a new dimension. To begin with, Candace Allen transferred from a school downtown to my elementary school in North Stamford. I was no longer the lone black child in the school. At first, I was worried about this prospect, thinking that the racial politics within the school would shift. With just me, there was no threat to the status quo. Would the white families at Hoyt consider that two black children equaled an invasion?

I actually knew Candy before she came to my school. When Candy was seven, my mother had spotted her riding her bicycle down the street from our town's famed Bloomingdale's Department Store. Candy was distinctive with her long legs and thick wavy brown hair, which was maintained in braids that lay on her back in two plats on each shoulder.

When Mom got home that afternoon after spotting Candy, she called Ellen Dickerson, a close friend who had lived in Stamford for many years, and learned that the girl's name was Candace Allen. Her father, Edward, was a dentist, her mother, Dee, a social worker. Candy, as it turned out, was the same age as I was and had a younger brother, Eddie, who was David's age. Mom couldn't have been more pleased with her find.

Ever since our move to the suburbs, Mom had been eager for David and me to have a close friend who was black, like Jackie had Bradley Gordon. The Gordons had moved east from Pasadena in 1956 when Dad opened a men's clothing store on 125th Street and recruited Jack to help manage it. Jack and Rudy Gordon lived in New York City and were happy to send their only child to spend summers with us in Stamford. We considered Bradley our adopted brother.

Not long after the first sighting, Mom had contacted Candy's mother and the two had arranged for us to meet. We were still in the awkward stage of early friendship when the Allens moved to a neighborhood a few miles from ours and Candy was enrolled at Hoyt.

The first day of class I twisted in my seat anxiously. I saved Candy a seat right next to me and kept watching the door for her arrival. Finally, Candy was escorted into our classroom by the principal. As our eyes and smiles met, my concerns faded. For the first time, I could look at one of my classmates and see a similarity.

It didn't take me long to realize that Candy was one of the smartest kids in the class. I marveled at her ability to stand in front of the room and rattle off the times tables. She didn't seem intimidated by the rows of white faces staring back at her. When Candy showed me her report card with all A's, I promoted her to the status of genius. Even Christy didn't get straight A's. I was holding steady to a B average myself.

The entrance of Candy into my life meant that the exclusivity that Christy and I had cherished no longer existed. It just so happened to fall at a point in our lives when the culturally imposed racial barriers of prepubescence were becoming more obvious. Boys and girls were beginning to play the early mating games and question the wisdom of playing co-ed football. The insults the two sexes exchanged were mixed with whispering and pointing as they identified the object of their affection. Notes were sent during class and hearts were drawn in notebooks. Daydreaming was considered the norm.

That same year, Chubby Checker came out with the "twist," a beat so enticing that it got my brother Jackie onto the dance floor. I was his first test. He grabbed me as I came in from school and pulled me into the living room just as "Come on let's twist again" blasted out through the living room speakers. Jackie and I swung our hips, twisted our feet, and flailed our arms wildly to the beat. We laughed and twisted some more. He must have been rehearsing for a party or something because he wanted to play that tune a dozen times until we got the moves right. It was such fun.

Our bodies had begun changing and my friends and I closely monitored each other's progress in the growth department. The first signs of budding breasts were met with squeals of delight. Boys suddenly became more interesting than touch football and the prospect of kissing and going to parties became the priority.

One object of our preteen fantasy was our fifth grade teacher. It was the first time we'd had a male teacher and all the girls seemed to have a crush on him. Instinctively, I knew that his whiteness and my blackness made even an innocent crush off limits. Still, I found myself longing for his attention, just like the other girls.

Since our elementary school did not have room for a sixth grade, our graduated fifth grade class left Hoyt and was sent to a much larger school for one year. There was no longer a single class for each grade. Candy, Christy, and I were placed in separate classes, a precursor to the tracking system of junior and senior high.

Around the same time, my mother, a recent master's degree graduate of the New York University School of Nursing, accepted a full-time job as a psychiatric nurse. I was selfishly nervous about how our lives would change as a result of Mom's new job. My mother tried to arrange it so that every detail would be covered. Willette continued to live with us during the week and my grandmother on my mother's side moved from Los Angeles to live with us as well. Grandma could drive us to and from our activities when my mother wasn't able to and could be at home to assure the smooth running of the house.

Having a working mother gave Candy and me something else in common and it also set us further apart from the other kids at school. Christy's mother was at home when we got off the bus, offering us snacks and listening to the details of our day. It was a luxury that I, too, had shared for the first five years of elementary school. I noticed friends' eyebrows going up disapprovingly when I mentioned that my mother had got a job. I tried to withhold judgment. I assumed that it would be okay because I had noticed that Candy didn't complain much unless her mother was late picking her up or couldn't attend some function that was being held during the day. And, initially, Dad was good about the change. With Chock Full O'Nuts, the civil rights movement, and golf, his post-baseball life was satisfying and full, so Mom's working did not seem to be a problem.

In January of 1962, I turned twelve and for my birthday I had a sleep-over. My girlfriends and I were camped out on the lower level of the house listening to 45s, dancing and talking, when Mom came downstairs looking upset. She asked Candy to come upstairs with her. My friends and I were distracted by my mother's actions, but we quickly returned to our activities. After a while Candy returned with my mother at her side. Mom gathered us together and told us that Candy's mother had died earlier in the evening.

At our age, death was associated with old age, car accidents, and heart attacks. Candy's mother had been young, healthy, and did not die in an automobile accident. We sat in silence listening as Mom talked. Mrs. Allen had been rushed to the emergency room after suddenly becoming very sick. She died mysteriously, shortly after admission. Terrified, realizing that it could have happened to any of us, I felt at a loss—not knowing what to say to Candy or how to behave.

It was strange to think of going to Candy's house and not see-ing Mrs. Allen. I remembered being there the day I started my period for the first time. Candy and I had just come in from play-

ing touch football. I went into the bathroom and within seconds
screamed. Candy came running and we both peered with fear and
embarrassment as I pointed at the blood in the toilet. I didn't want
Candy to ask her mother for Kotex but we had no choice. After
giving me words of encouragement and sanitary napkins, Mrs.
Allen called my mother and gave her the news. My mother was so
pleased that I had technically entered womanhood that I quickly
got beyond my embarrassment and enjoyed the new status that
came with the biological change.

My other memory of Mrs. Allen was observing her in the
tedious process of brushing Candy's hair. My friend would scream
in protest with each stroke. When Mrs. Allen tired of her daughter's theatrics, she would take the hairbrush and gently bop Candy
on the head. That would shut her up. We all worried about the
management of Candy's thick wavy hair when her mom died.
There was no way that Dr. Allen could assume that task alone. The
solution lay in taking a grateful Candy to the beauty shop and having her braids chopped off.

While the death of Candy's mother threw us off balance, the
change junior high would make in my life eventually absorbed all
my attention. Like my friends, I was tired of being a little girl and
no one could have convinced us that junior high would not make
us grown-ups. As sixth grade came to a close, I turned the volume
all the way up on Gary "U.S." Bonds singing our summer theme
song "School Is Out" and danced around the living room in my
house in anticipation of a new life in junior high school.

Just as I was vacillating between the old world of a tomboy and
the new world of a teenager, Mom came home with news that
would sway me back toward childhood play. We were, at last, getting a horse! I was so excited that I didn't care that our newest pet
was actually given to David.

My mother and father had met a woman at a dinner party in
Greenwich whose son had outgrown his horse. In the course of
the conversation, my mother told the lady about her ten-year-old
son and his love of horses. I, too, loved horses and, at the age of
eight, had started asking Mom to buy me a horse. Mom bought

me horse books to study and took me to a horse show in Danbury but that was as far as we went. This was an unexpected gift.

Mom, knowing that maintaining a horse was a huge responsibility, sat David and me down and explained that he would be our responsibility. My parents would find someone to give us horseback riding lessons and build us a barn and stable on an unused portion of our property. We would have to feed, water, exercise, and maintain his stable. David and I happily agreed to all the terms.

When Diamond arrived we discovered that he was a black-and-white pony that stood about fourteen hands high and weighed roughly fifteen hundred pounds. In the winter he had a long thick coat and looked twice his size. David and I saddled our new acquisition and my brother hoisted his slim body onto its back. The horse made the most awful sounds, alerting us to his displeasure, and then reared up several times as we had seen horses do on television. It took persistence to finally get the irate animal controlled enough so that we could ride him.

David and I took turns exercising Diamond. While Diamond was tamed by our determination and skill, he remained an evil horse. David's job was to water and feed Diamond before he left for school each morning. Usually he would do so still wearing his school clothes. Making their regular trip to the lake for water, Diamond, depending upon his mood, would on occasion continue into the lake, forcing David to take an unwelcome swim. David would have to sneak back into the house to change clothes before Mom discovered his folly. Other times, Diamond would drag David or me under low-lying branches, or rear up, all in an effort to shed his load. Once, in full gallop, he forced me against a mailbox. First, I heard my pant leg tear, then I was hit by this excruciating pain. Somehow our romance with horse ownership wasn't all we thought it would be.

From the time we entered Dolan Junior High, Christy, Candy, and I encountered challenges that we hadn't anticipated. To begin with, I tested poorly on the admissions test and was placed in one of the lowest academic groupings. Each group was assigned a number that fell somewhere between one and ten. It didn't take much to figure out that Group 7–7, the one I was assigned to, was for the below-average students. Christy and Candy were both placed in the accelerated classes, and I was embarrassed by my ascribed status as a mediocre student.

The biggest change for me as we entered junior high was the growing importance of boys in our lives. The girls in our classes and on the school bus talked endlessly about them, many of whom still played side by side with us in our seasonal ball games. Even Christy had a story to tell. Candy and I were at a loss, desperately wanting to share in these conversations since our hormones were stirring as well. But we were hopeless outsiders. There was one black boy in our junior high: he was too short for Candy and not the least bit attractive to me. So on the sidelines we sat, miserably listening as the girls cooed over their latest crushes and planned secret weekend meetings.

It wasn't long before Christy was asked out on her first date. In a panic, Christy and I went to the Stamford Library to get a book on sexuality because we realized that neither of us knew how to kiss a boy. After searching through the stacks, pulling out book after book that had some vague reference to dating, we finally found a treasure. Feeling brave, I checked out the book with my library card, stuffed it into my book bag, and we headed home on the bus.

An hour later, we were safely behind my bedroom door with the book turned to page fifty-seven trying to decipher a diagram on how to kiss. As I read the passages, Christy walked off the steps as depicted in the diagram. Then, she read, and I walked off the steps that led up to the kiss.

"This is silly," I finally admitted, falling onto my bed with laughter.

"Can you imagine counting to five and realizing that the boy was still a foot away?" Christy added before flopping next to me, joining in the relief of laughter.

"I've had enough of this," I concluded.

"Me, too. I'm ready for this date. Probably won't get kissed anyway," Christy agreed.

"Remember our discussions about sex with our moms?" I reminded Christy.

"Yeah, why?"

"Well, I don't remember kissing coming up in my discussions. How about you?" I asked, curious about why it was so mysterious.

"No, me either."

Our introductory talk on womanhood had occurred when we turned twelve. It was a prerequisite to a scheduled Girl Scout meeting devoted to our blossoming sexuality. The troop leaders asked the mothers to sit down with their daughters for a private discussion before the scheduled group discussion.

Mom and I had sat on the sofa in the living room one afternoon when everyone else was out of the house. I had read the booklet that our troop leader had given to us so I was marginally prepared. Mom opened the conversation with the least threatening topic: the menstrual cycle. I found the menstrual cycle clinical. Conception was far more interesting, and the topic of sex really piqued my curiosity. My mother had been really cool and relaxed about the whole thing, including mentioning that sex within marriage was beautiful. I had listened for details like how to kiss, but Mom left the particulars up to my imagination. I was too embarrassed to ask for clarification of little understood points. It was just too hard to imagine something so adult happening to me. Not wanting Mom to think I didn't know the stuff, I listened quietly, throwing in a sigh and a "I know, Mom," a couple of times, because twelve-year-olds know everything. When Mom hit on a truly foreign topic, I nodded to let her know I understood, even if I really didn't.

Christy and I had agreed prior to our mother-daughter talks that we would compare notes afterward. The first opportunity I got, I called Christy on the phone. She reported the details of her discussion, which seemed pretty close to mine except that her mom hadn't talked about sex. So, we were left to discover the finer details of this mysterious lovemaking on our own.

After Christy and I had thoroughly studied kissing from the text and role-played, we acknowledged that Christy was ready for her first date. I was envious of my friend but didn't tell her. I didn't understand the envy or my feelings of inadequacy. I only knew that my best friend was about to have an experience that I wished I were having.

As Saturday grew close, Christy's confidence began to fade. Naturally she turned to me for help. We devised a plan whereby I could provide moral support yet remain in the background. On the morning of the date, we talked on the phone and agreed that Christy would call me as she was leaving her house heading for the bus stop. She and her date were going downtown to an afternoon movie and would have to pass my house on their way. My job was to time their passing so that I would walk out of my driveway shortly after. The timing worked perfectly, except that somewhere between my house and the bus stop I no longer felt good about our plan.

As I walked ten feet or so behind Christy, on the other side of the street, I watched her talking nervously with this boy. My pace slowed, my mind wandered, but my eyes remained fixed on the boy and girl walking in front of me. It was like one of those tests where you're asked to identify all the things that are wrong with the picture. At first you pick out all the obvious things like the bird upside down on the tree branch and the girl with only one boot on. Then it hits you that the little girl doesn't have a ribbon on her second ponytail and there's no doorknob on the front door of the house. You circle the weird things you've identified and continue to search for others.

Well, it was obvious that Christy and her date were white and I was black. We were not a threesome. But the discomfort continued to nag at me. I found myself wondering if I would ever be asked out on a date or if boys would someday find me attractive. My father had been telling me since I was a little girl that I was pretty and he was a man, I told myself reassuringly. I felt better. My brothers hadn't said one way or the other. They were never any real help. My mother, grandmother, and Willette had all told me that I was pretty. I had lots of reason to be hopeful. But I also knew that my circumstances would have to change if I was ever going to prove my desirability.

I was still trying to figure out what that change would be as I arrived at the bus stop a few minutes after Christy. The bus pulled up right on schedule. I climbed on the bus, handed the driver twenty-five cents, and took a seat behind my friend.

There were only a handful of people on the bus. I looked around and noticed one other black person. She appeared to be about my mother's age. On her lap was a shopping bag. Her hair was tied up tight in a painted scarf. I assumed that she was a house-keeper on her way home. We smiled at each other.

My mind returned to solving the remainder of the puzzle. It all seemed so unfair when I realized that I could not really share this experience with the girl I had always considered my best friend. The things that we had in common no longer mattered. We were at a major turning point and neither of us could fully share the experience with the other. Suddenly, her white skin and my black skin made an insurmountable difference. I was beginning to feel humiliated. I realized that I could not describe to my "best friend" the pain of being an outsider, nor could I share in her excitement over the details of her first date. And this was only the beginning. I knew that there would be more dates, more moments of rejec-tion. Angered by the inequity, I wanted no part of this white world that surrounded me.

I had a flashback to the first time that I saw *The Jackie Robinson Story* that rainy afternoon at Camp Holloway. Up until that moment I had been able to separate Christy from the white peo-ple in the movie who had called my dad names. Now the lines were blurred.

I thought of our family discussion about the Little Rock Nine. Dad had talked of the children's courage and determination. Even after the students got into Central High, the harassment contin-ued. The students were threatened with expulsion if they publi-cized the harassment or caused any further trouble. Minnie Brown was eventually kicked out. She accepted a $1,050 scholarship to attend the New Lincoln School, a private, interracial institution in New York. She came to New York accompanied by her mother and enrolled. I hadn't heard any more about her. I wondered if she was in college now. I even wondered if integration should be a goal.

I thought of how racially separated Stamford, Connecticut, was. The only time that I saw large numbers of black people was when I was on the west side of Stamford near the projects. I thought of how much I disliked not going to school with or living near other black children. I cursed my parents' decision to move to an all-white community. The country was beautiful and all, but I yearned for a connectedness to people like me.

Not sure what to do next, I winked at Christy as she got off at her stop but didn't budge from my seat. I stared out of the window as the bus continued on its route. We came to the last stop. There were just me and the bus driver left on the bus. The bus driver turned around and reminded me that we had come to the end of the line. I got up and paid him another twenty-five cents then sat back down. He turned the bus around and headed back toward the northern end of town.

At home, I retreated to my room. I read, slept for a while, looked over my homework, then, around seven o'clock, my fingers moved from memory as I dialed Christy's number. Mrs. Joyce answered the phone.

"Hello, Mrs. Joyce. May I speak with Christy?"

"Yes, Sharon—hold on a minute. Christy?" I heard her call out. "Sharon is on the phone." I heard the familiar voice, took a deep breath.

"Hi. I was just getting ready to call you."

"How was the movie?" I was nervous, still thinking through my words.

"It was stupid. What are you doing? Want to come over?" She asked, innocent of what was really on my mind.

"Can't. Ah, Christy—I've been thinking. I can't keep being your best friend," I stammered out.

"What are you talking about?" Christy was confused.

"I'm calling to say that we can no longer be best friends." I repeated myself, seemingly certain of the need to end the friendship. It was so definitive. A move made in a moment of anger. Not

68   SHARON ROBINSON

so much at Christy but at the inequity that she represented. The world was becoming clearer. At thirteen going on fourteen, who knows where that cold determination came from. I didn't know then and still don't have all the answers. I only knew that this dating issue was the great divider and in order to be a player I would have to associate with more black kids.

After Christy and I hung up, there were no return phone calls, no change of heart on my part, nor any intervention from our parents. Mom and Dad did not like my conclusion, but accepted the decision, and sat down with me to talk about solutions to my dilemma. The answer, as they saw it, lay with membership in Jack & Jill.

Jack & Jill is a national organization designed to provide social and service outlets for middle-class black children. Families interested in membership for their children must apply. Acceptance is based on a number of factors: the mother's ability to be active, the father's career, the family's social standing, to name a few. While our membership was never in question, my mother told me of their reputation from her childhood of excluding families whose skin color was too dark. In the fifties, the prejudice remained, but it was not the sole deciding factor: parents' profession, marital status, and address were given equal consideration. By the time Candy and I were active, the ranks of the organization had swelled with kids who could boast of their father being a doctor, lawyer, or corporate executive.

The Jack & Jill experience was not unique in the social structure of black society. Its earlier slant on membership dated back to shortly after slavery, when light-skinned blacks claimed a form of aristocracy which lasted until the turn of the century, when intermarriage with darker-skinned blacks from the full range of classes diluted the color caste and a black middle class evolved with emphasis on personal success and economic achievement. By the fifties, the old mulatto families and the black-skinned middle class were known collectively as the "black bourgeoisie," and it was from within this elitist group that Jack & Jill sought its members.

As new recruits, Candy and I had to prove to be good members by attending the monthly meetings, going on field trips, and participating in cultural affairs. As our first year in Jack & Jill came to a close our excitement mounted in anticipation of our first formal Jack & Jill dance. I remember the dress-up affair with amusement.

Billie Allen, Candy's aunt, invited us to Hempstead to shop for our outfits. This was perfect because we thought that Candy's actress aunt was so cool, and therefore anything she was involved in was extra special. The very idea of shopping in New York, even if it wasn't Manhattan, added to the intrigue of the upcoming event. Candy and I took the train by ourselves to Long Island. Billie met us at the Hempstead station and took us straight to a large shopping center nearby so that we would have a wide selection of stores. Once we were in the junior section of a large department store we found a plethora of party dresses. Aunt Billie let us loose to pick out our outfits. Candy fell in love with a white piqué dress with lilac irises on the lacy border of the skirt. I selected a yellow nylon-chiffon dress with puff sleeves and a princess neckline. Both dresses had full skirts that required multi-layered crinolines to do them justice. Mom had said no to high heels and Billie agreed. So Candy looked for blue flats but settled for white slippers. I found yellow ballerina slippers. To top our outfits off, we each got our first pair of sheer nylons.

The morning of the dance, Mom took Candy and me to the only black beauty shop in Stamford. We nearly died from the heat and fumes coming from burning hair and scalp grease. After five hours, Candy and I emerged with our freshly permed and styled hair. My mother was amused by our complaints and informed us that five hours was a small price to pay for beauty.

Later that evening, Billie drove in from Hempstead to escort us to the dance, watching discreetly from across the room until she realized that the dance would soon end and Candy and I had not yet set foot on the dance floor. Hoping to avert a disaster, she crossed the dance floor and coaxed and humored, even suggested that we ask a boy to dance. We didn't budge. Billie brightened as we watched a young boy headed in our direction. But the boy hadn't come to ask Candy or me to dance. He asked Billie to dance. Frustrated, and a little embarrassed, she tried diplomacy.

"I'm the chaperone, but here are two beautiful girls who would love to dance." His eyes shifted toward Candy and me and he must have decided that it wasn't worth it, because he moved on. Years later, I learned that Billie went after that boy and gave him exactly five minutes to find a friend, return to the two girls he had just rejected, and ask them to dance. All Candy and I knew was that the night was a success because our new shoes had hit the dance floor.

From our first semiformal to my first kiss, the summer of 1963 was filled with new experiences. Mom helped David and me pack for two weeks in a camp for children of Chock Full O'Nuts employees. With the exception of one session at a Girl Scout camp, I usually did not go to sleepaway camps during the summer, but this promised to be a unique experience. Dad speculated that more than half of the children would be black. Dad had also convinced Aunt Brenda and Uncle Chuck to send our cousins Rhoda and Kirk with us.

Mom and Dad drove us to the camp. It was set in the midst of tall evergreen trees high on a hill. Small cabins were nestled in the pine-covered wooded hills. Our car arrived about the same time as busloads of black children from Manhattan and its surrounding boroughs were also dropped off. Rhoda and I were housed in the same cabin, David and Kirk, in another. We each had a bunk bed and a sleeping bag. David and I adjusted almost immediately. This was not the case with our cousins. Rhoda cried for home every night. I felt sympathetic toward her for the first two nights, after that I just felt embarrassed. David said that Kirk cried each night, too. From his description it sounded as if he carried on worse than his twin sister. I was surprised that he didn't stop in the face of the merciless teasing from the other boys in his cabin. After several days of tearful telephone calls, Uncle Chuck and Aunt Brenda came to rescue their children. David and I stayed and enjoyed the remainder of the camp session.

The last evening of camp was, undeniably, one of the highlights of the two weeks. I had become quite friendly with Randy, a boy from the Bronx. Our last evening in camp, he walked me back to my cabin after the campfire. We promised to write to each other. As I turned to say good-bye to my new friend, whom I already missed, Randy bent down and kissed me on my lips. Just as I reached to kiss him back, as Christy and I had rehearsed, his tongue darted in and out of my mouth. I thought that I would vomit! I broke away from his embrace and ran into the cabin without looking back. I brushed my teeth repeatedly, trying to erase any memory of Randy's disgusting gesture. I was through with my friend. Suddenly, I was glad to be going home and hoped that Randy's bus would pull out before I got up in the morning. The next morning I felt better and told a couple of the girls in my cabin about the kiss. We had a good laugh and then they explained to me about tongue kissing. Randy was human again and I had to admit being happy to have finally been kissed. With new confidence, I left camp ready to tackle my final year in junior high.

Inspired by Maria in the movie *West Side Story,* I insisted on taking Spanish the fall of ninth grade. This was a problem for my guidance counselor because I was assigned to Group 9–7. Foreign languages were allowed only for students in groups above four. Remembering the misunderstood Maria, I held my ground as if the Romance language held the key to my salvation, or at least to my first love.

My guidance counselor's efforts to convince me that I was not ready for a foreign language fell on deaf ears. Unwilling to accept her decision, I went home and complained to my mother. Incensed, my mother stormed into the school to stand up for me. Her presence made the difference. I was moved up three groups and allowed to take Introductory Spanish.

For the first time, I felt challenged. My grades and class participation improved to meet the higher expectations. I was, however, disappointed to learn that there was only one Puerto Rican boy in the class. When my teacher asked for volunteers to tutor the recent immigrant, I jumped at the opportunity, thinking that maybe this was my "Tony." Well, love was not our destiny, but his English improved and my learning of Spanish was enhanced.

More important, for the first time in my school years, I thought of myself as a good student. It was not the same as being smart, but it was certainly better than being average.

After that awkward first Jack & Jill dance, Candy and I moved with deliberate speed onto the party circuit. With Candy's cousins in Hempstead and mine in Roosevelt, we received and accepted invitations to Jack & Jill–sponsored parties in Nassau County as well as in New Jersey. When we weren't in Long Island, Candy and I gave parties in our homes. My parents welcomed my friends, and in turn my friends were only too happy to take advantage of the many dark secluded spots on our property.

In preparation, Candy and I would turn the downstairs into a party hall. A few red lights strategically placed, 45s by Marvin Gaye, Martha Reeves & the Vandellas, Mary Wells, Stevie Wonder, the Supremes, and the Temptations stacked by the record player, chips, homemade brownies, and punch, and we were ready.

My parents were always at home when we had a party. Dad would make a sweep of the downstairs before it began and during the party he remained upstairs in the living room while the music vibrated from below. Occasionally, Dad ventured downstairs after a party was under way just to check to make sure that the lights were on and we were behaving. I remember a lesson he taught me during a picnic we had at our house for visiting African students. I had turned it into a party and we were having a good time dancing to the music when I saw my father come down the steps. I was wrapped around some boy during a slow dance. My arms encircled his waist. As the record ended, Dad signaled to me. The frown on his face was a warning. He didn't really look angry, just annoyed. He talked softly to avoid embarrassing me, but firmly enough so that I knew he was serious. I got the message: too close. He demonstrated with his arms the proper two-step position. Dad wasn't much of a dancer. He only knew the two-step. I wanted to laugh at the idea of his instructing me in the appropriate dance form, but I understood it was more about propriety than form.

For most kids my age, curfew was midnight and parents provided the transportation. This was always a little tricky at my house because couples would often sneak out into the grounds and find dark places to neck. Since I wouldn't know who was in or out of the house, when a parent arrived at the front door to pick up one of the girls I would try to get to the door before my parents and politely suggest to the parent that they wait in the car and I would send their daughter outside. Then I would fly downstairs in a mad search. If I could not find the girl in the house, I'd head out the back and run down the hill calling out the girl's name. Girls would come running from every direction even if their name hadn't been called fearing discovery if they didn't emerge quickly. We could enter the house through the downstairs and come up the steps and no one over the age of eighteen would be the wiser.

As the end of ninth grade approached, my friends and I focused on high school, but before I could graduate from junior high, I had one more battle to fight. The enemy was the mandatory class dance. With disdain, I remembered the one from the year before. For the last two periods of the day, classes were canceled. We filed into the gym by homeroom and lined up along the wall. At first no one wanted to dance. But by the end of the two hours, I began to imagine that everyone had danced except for Candy and me. I reasoned this to be a racial issue and consequently I resented the forced participation, especially given the odds of some white boy asking Candy or me to dance. Since my encounter with Randy over the summer, I had confidence in my attractiveness and decided it was time to act out my displeasure with the imposed period of socialization. On the morning of the dance, I woke up and lay in bed planning what I would wear, since I had decided that my outfit would be my signal of rebellion. I pulled out my despised plaid skirt first and "matched" it with a floral blouse. I completed the outfit with bobby socks and sneakers. Smiling at my misfit image in the mirror, I emerged from my room. I was so blind with cockiness that I nearly ran smack into Jackie. He took one look at me and asked where I thought I was going looking like that. There, I thought to myself, it worked.

Content, I headed off to the bus stop. The kids looked at me strangely but didn't comment. At school some of my classmates laughed, some stared, and others didn't seem to notice. It didn't matter; I was happy and in control. The sixth-period bell rang and we headed off to the gym to party. I strutted into the room. Of course, no one asked me to dance that year either. But I really didn't care. That time it was my choice, and as far as I was concerned I had won.

While I was fighting a comparatively silly battle in junior high, all around me the temperatures were rising in the battle for civil rights. A year earlier, my family, along with hundreds of thousands of others, traveled to the 1963 March on Washington. Early in the day I fainted from the extreme heat and massive crowds. Thankfully, I recovered in time to hear Dr. King.

That same summer my father spearheaded a New York fundraising drive for the Southern Christian Leadership Conference. Several churches in the South had been bombed in protest against SCLC's work. There was a big affair at the Apollo Theater in Harlem and Dad had convinced Mr. Black of Chock Full O'Nuts to give money. Governor Rockefeller personally gave ten thousand dollars. Satisfied with the success of the first fund-raiser, Mom and Dad planned a second: a jazz concert on the lawn of our Stamford home with the proceeds earmarked to provide a bail fund for jailed civil rights' activists. My brothers and I swelled with excitement when we learned that Dr. Martin Luther King Jr. would be coming to our home! We volunteered to help get the house and grounds ready. The day of the concert, friends arrived early with platters of fried chicken, salads, cakes, cookies, and brownies to add to the feast that my mother and grandmother had prepared. Dad stayed on the phone right up to the last moment, working out the details with the performers and Dr. King's staff. Everything had to be perfect.

At the suggestion of sunrise, Mom roused the troops by blasting spirituals. Jackie, David, and I bathed and made our beds so that our rooms would be neat before the artists and guests arrived. It was a clear summer day and the tent that had been erected the day before sat in green-and-white-striped splendor at the base of the hill.

My parents opened their home, surrendered their grounds, and

welcomed the public. Dad, determined that his lawn was going to
survive this day, decided to take personal responsibility for directing the parking of the cars.

I was surprised that Dr. King's arrival was met without ceremony. He greeted my parents warmly and Dad made the formal
introductions. We stood in mute witness, not sure what to say to
this famous man. Ordinarily, I wasn't thrown by celebrities, but Dr.
King was different. He had a deep, seductive Southern accent and
standing in his presence was as close to God as I figured I would
ever get.

The day proceeded smoothly. People came, the music flowed
throughout the afternoon, and Dad said we made lots of money.
Dr. King moved easily among the people sprawled on the lawns.
As the day wound down, Dad and Dr. King thanked the people for
coming and he made a quiet exit. While the details of the day
remain fuzzy in my mind, the impact has lasted. We had been listening to our parents for years, learning about our history second-
hand. This day was special because it made us active participants.
No, we hadn't picketed or fought off dogs, but we had helped raise
money to support an aspect of the movement.

But just as Dad's fame had ushered us into front-row seats on
the steps of the Lincoln Memorial to hear Dr. King deliver his "I
Have a Dream" speech that August day, so had it put us on the
front line of so much that was happening nationwide. Seven years
of retirement from baseball had not lessened that fact of our lives—
it escalated it.

The same year as Dr. King's speech, Governor George Wallace
literally made a federal case of keeping two black students from
entering the University of Alabama as a huge battalion of soldiers
in battle gear with rifles drawn stood in wait; Medgar Evers, the
NAACP's crusader, was shot dead in the driveway of his home
while local officials made a hero of his arrogant killer; days after the
inspiring multiracial "high" of the March on Washington, reality
killed four young girls when a pro-segregationist's bomb tore the
roof off their Birmingham church; President Kennedy publicly
mourned the girls, condemning the violence on national televi-

sion, and within weeks personally joined the growing list of hate's victims when he was killed in Dallas. Amazingly, all of this happened in six months—May to November 1963, as I completed junior high.

In the fall of 1964, I entered Stamford High School with a mixture of excitement and trepidation. It had been ten years since the *Brown v. Board of Education* ruling, and Connecticut was finally taking action to correct the racial imbalance in the schools. The plan was to be implemented for tenth grade. Over the summer, construction on the new senior high school closer to my house had been completed. Candy and I assumed it would soon be our home. But because the Board of Education was working out the busing plan, my friends and I didn't know until late in the summer which of the two public schools we'd be assigned to.

Just before the opening day of school, the *Stamford Advocate* printed the busing plan. Cascade Road was divided in half. I was disappointed to learn that my side of the street had been assigned to the ancient Stamford High. My disappointment turned to relief when I read further and realized that Candy had suffered the same fate.

Rippowam, the nearby high school, was a contemporary structure covered with green tile and lots of windows, and was considered a country club. Stamford High, an enormous red-brick building with windows that were divided in such a way that they looked like bars, was called the jail. Rumors abounded that the halls of Stamford High were filled with opposing switchblade-carrying gangs. Our friends used the rumors to their advantage, quietly hoping that Candy and I would fight the decision and join them at Rippowam.

The high school arrangement was all we had talked about for weeks. Now, with our assignments out in the open, the talk got more serious. Should we accept our placements quietly? It was a dilemma for me because I wanted to be in a school with more black kids, and yet I wanted to go to the new school. Twanda Bowers, Barbara Smith, and Natalie Dickerson, our friends from

Jack & Jill, were no help. They were going to Rippowam and kept pressuring Candy and me to get our parents to change our high school assignment. For me, fighting the decision meant to enforce integration would have been the antithesis of my training and socialization. I just couldn't do it, and neither could Candy. So we accepted the decision and on the first day of school boarded a yellow school bus and headed past Rippowam toward downtown to Stamford High. I took a seat, and while maintaining a conversation with the girl sitting next to me, silently wondered what must be going through the minds of the white kids on the bus.

At the other end of town, the black students boarded their buses as well. The usual anxiety that comes with a new experience was heightened by the uncertainties of the experiment. As we stepped off our respective buses at the entrance to Stamford High, my attention was drawn to the groups of black students milling around the entrance to the school. We eyed each other cautiously, not really sure what to expect. We filed into the imposing structure and reported to our homeroom with the inappropriate chatter that comes when one is nervous.

Once inside the building, our class groupings and course assignments were given to us and we forgot about first-day nerves. There were two givens that I had come to understand about the tracking system. One was that the majority of the black students would be placed in the technical tracks and, second, that Candy would be the exception. Candy, as I had anticipated, was placed in the gifted class. My placement in 10–2 was a welcomed surprise. I realized that if I hadn't taken Spanish in the ninth grade, the option of college could have been denied me simply because I wouldn't have had the proper prerequisites. I was lucky. Many of my black classmates were not as fortunate.

With a world of new possibilities in front of me, I soon became enamored of the idea of being a cheerleader. I wanted to wear one of those short skirts, turn flips in the air, and learn to do perfect splits. I even went so far as to show up at the gym during the try-outs, but I took one look at all those white girls and decided that I didn't fit in. Candy, who had been practicing for months and was proficient in doing a split, was selected to cheerlead while I signed up for the girl's basketball, soccer, and track teams.

The decision not to pursue cheerleading was not completely my choice, but I quickly learned that sports, especially basketball, was a great way to get to know the other black girls in my school. At least half of the team was black. I was a good athlete and easily got a spot on the team as a guard, which was important since I couldn't make a basket to save my life. Part of my problem was the fact that I was still terribly nearsighted yet wouldn't wear my glasses. As a guard, I could pretty much find my way around the court in a blur and keep track of who I was assigned to guard. I was also a fast runner, and in my sophomore and junior years placed second to Candy in the high jump competition. Just as it had been for so many others before me, sports became an avenue for me to move into another world. High school, I decided, was looking pretty good.

6

Politics and Race

I was barely through my first semester of high school when my cousin Chuckie phoned, feverish with news. "Your father is an Uncle Tom!"

"He is not!" I shouted into the phone. I was fifteen at the time and not sure of all the implications of the term, but I knew it was a put-down and I wasn't about to let my cousin get away with insulting my father even if I didn't completely understand it. Chuckie's words still stung, but pride would not allow me to let him know how much.

It was obvious to me even then that Dad didn't deserve the name-calling; no one did. My father never sold his soul or his people. Even if I was not yet old enough to let it roll off my back as easily as it rolled off other people's tongues, I knew that in those times, we needed to be unified, not attacking each other. And while my father did make mistakes, those armed with rocks like the words "Uncle Tom" were those who neither knew my father nor the glass houses of their own collective history.

Before Chuckie could even respond to my vehement denial, I asked, fearing the answer, "What makes you say that?" Maybe my father had said or done something outrageous. I knew that he was capable of being very outspoken and controversial. I remembered all the loud arguing that would go on after Thanksgiving dinner. It was as much a part of the day's rituals as watching football on television. Chuckie's mother, Brenda, was the loudest and most self-righteous of the group. She and Dad would jump in each other's faces trying to get their opinions heard over the shouting. My cousins and I learned after the first few confrontations not to take their loud words seriously. Their political arguments were part of the day's fun. At the start of the fireside chat, my cousins, brothers, and I would head for the playroom.

Chuckie said that he had overheard his mother talking to his dad, my mother's brother, and anyway, "He's a Republican, isn't he?" This wasn't really a question. This was a charge.

"I'm not sure," I had to admit. Chuckie had me there. "I'll call you back." I hung up quickly realizing that I needed facts.

I thought back to the first time I recognized party affiliation as defining of character, beliefs, personal choice. I was in the fifth grade and my teacher took a vote before the Kennedy/Nixon election of 1960. He divided us according to how our parents were voting. My mother was a faithful Democrat, supporting John F. Kennedy. At the start of the 1960 presidential campaign season my father had been a strong supporter of the liberal Democrat Hubert Humphrey. Humphrey was strong on both labor and civil rights issues. Senator Kennedy, on the other hand, was better financed but had a shaky voting record on civil rights legislation. In 1957, he had voted to weaken the civil rights bill and received strong endorsement from Governor John Patterson of Alabama, an arch-segregationist. Kennedy beat Humphrey in the primaries and became the nominee for the Democratic party.

The Kennedy camp assumed that my father would maintain his Democratic affiliation and automatically support JFK. The two sat down in a private meeting. My father came away still distrustful of Kennedy because the candidate did not look him directly in the eyes. My father ultimately supported Richard Nixon, believing that it was important to have blacks affiliated with both parties so that their vote would not be taken for granted. As a registered Independent, my father was able to work on either side. The decision to support Nixon lost my father his job as a columnist for the *New York Post* and he was placed on an unpaid leave of absence from Chock Full O'Nuts. While campaigning for the Republican candidate, Richard Nixon, Dad became disenchanted and several times considered dropping out but chose to keep campaigning on his behalf. Ultimately, it was the response of the two candidates to the jailing of Martin Luther King Jr. that swayed the black community in favor of Kennedy. The Kennedy group stepped in and worked on behalf of his release. Nixon refused, in spite of the urging of his black supporters, my father included, to use his influence to get King out of jail. King was released and the black community credited JFK.

At ten, I did not really understand politics. I wanted Kennedy to win because he represented youth, new direction, vitality, hope— not to mention good looks. But my views didn't matter and the teacher insisted that I go on the Republican side, my father's side.

After the class activity, I went home and pleaded with my father to switch sides for my sake. I even tried telling him that he was probably the only black person in American not supporting Kennedy. I didn't know this to be true but it felt that way. This wasn't the first time my father had taken a controversial stance that seemed counter to the mood of black people. During Dad's baseball days he was increasingly asked to comment on things outside of baseball. In 1949, this extended to testimony before the House Un-American Activities Committee in response to a statement made by Paul Robeson that blacks would not fight Russia for America. Dad, caught between his belief that there were in effect two battles raging—one against foreign enemies and the other against domestic foes—felt that the black man must fight both and testified to such. The actual words of his text were lost in the effort by others to pit one black man against another.

In the Kennedy versus Nixon election I was old enough to be aware of the divisiveness of Dad's decision. I learned more about my father's stubbornness when even the pleas of his only daughter could not budge him. Dad tried to get me to understand his side. With him everything was principle. He told me of his personal interview with John F. Kennedy and the fact that he did not try to disguise his lack of understanding of issues affecting the black community. Nixon, my father insisted, had a positive voting record on several pieces of civil rights legislation and was at least a known entity. Kennedy was untested. Thankfully, Kennedy won that round, so the country was spared Nixon for a few more years. Three years later, President Kennedy gave an impassioned televised speech that demonstrated his understanding and support for civil rights. After listening to his message, my father sent him a telegram that very night thanking him for emerging as a committed and forthright president. He went further and acknowledged Kennedy's courage and wisdom on civil rights in his column in the *Amsterdam News*.

I had been unsuccessful in 1960 in getting my father to switch to Kennedy, but I had been very proud of his ability to put his pride aside and admit he was wrong when the situation called for an honest response. Here I was four years later, knowing of my father's stubbornness, unsure of how to handle this name-calling situation. I couldn't ask Dad if he was an Uncle Tom. For some reason, I couldn't even ask my parents what an Uncle Tom was. I knew that this was more than an issue of Republican versus Democrat, this was about not allowing others to define you.

I went back to my room and lay across my bed trying to come up with a way to pose my question without it seeming like an attack. I decided to go directly to my father and ask him if he was a Republican. If he said yes, then I felt it would add credibility to Chuckie's label.

I held my breath as I awaited my father's answer. He paused, looking pensive. "Yes." Dad seemed to admit it. Then, he went on.

"I'm a black man first. I don't want either the Democrats or Republicans to take black people for granted. So, I register as an Independent and that allows me the freedom to support which candidate I feel will fight for laws that will help our communities."

I felt a little confused because my father's response did not clarify my real question. But I was also relieved because it did not con-

firm it. Dad wasn't a man of a lot of words. He didn't expand on
our discussion and I didn't push the issue.

I was a little wiser than I was in 1960 and even more eager to
put things into my own version of perspective. I knew that 1964
had been a difficult year for my father. His health was failing him.
He had been taking insulin for eight years to control his adult-
onset diabetes but it had been increasingly unstable. Dad's poor
health wasn't his only problem. Since his campaign for Nixon,
Dad's reputation in the black community had taken a hard hit. He
was considered a conservative by many. At the start of 1964, my
father resigned from Chock Full O'Nuts and within months
accepted a position as assistant campaign manager for Nelson
Rockefeller, the liberal Republican candidate for president.

Later that same year Dad invited us to accompany him to the
1964 Republican Convention. Mom, Dad, David, and I flew to
San Francisco and had our station wagon driven out West. After
the convention, Dad promised us the opportunity to see the
northern half of America by car. What I didn't realize when
Chuckie made his phone call and I asked my father about his party
affiliation was that my father underwent a huge change in his
political direction in 1964. Dad was not an official delegate to the
convention, but he had access to the floor as a member of
Governor Rockefeller's campaign staff. Rockefeller's opponent at
the convention, Senator Barry Goldwater, was the hero of the
Southern conservatives.

While my father attended the convention, Mom showed David
and me around San Francisco, and after the convention was over,
we got into our black station wagon and for a week we were a
relaxed unified family again. Dad even let me steer the car through
a stretch of desert.

We stayed at the Grand Canyon and Yosemite National Park and
spent a few hours at Governor Rockefeller's ranch in Wyoming.
Dad and the governor sat on the porch in rocking chairs talking
politics. Later my father told us that their conversation centered
around the convention, which they both felt had been a farce. Dad
told us of how the Goldwater galleries booed so loudly that
Rockefeller could not be heard when he spoke in defense of the

minority plank condemning by name the Communist Party, the John Birch Society, and the Ku Klux Klan. When the party went on to nominate Barry Goldwater, it signaled a shift to the right within the party and in the country.

Once again refusing to be pinned down, Dad informed Rockefeller that he was so frustrated by the transference of power among the Republicans that he planned to defect and campaign for Johnson.

Within weeks of the Republican Convention, President Johnson signed the Civil Rights Act of 1964. Eleven days before the signing, civil rights workers Michael H. Schwerner, Andrew Goodman, and James E. Chaney were reported missing in Mississippi. On August 4, their bodies were found buried near Philadelphia, Mississippi. On July 18, 1964, a white patrolman had shot a fifteen-year-old black boy in the course of a routine arrest. And the next day a protest march in Harlem, New York, became a battle with the police, setting off a series of rebellions that exploded from Harlem to Rochester.

Fearing that the protests would cause a distraction from the critical elections and a white backlash against Johnson, Martin Luther King Jr., Whitney Young, Roy Wilkins, and A. Philip Randolph issued pleas, on behalf of their respective organizations, calling for a moratorium on demonstrations until after the elections. While it seemed improbable that Goldwater would capture the country and win the election, the black leadership didn't want to take that chance. They wanted all energy focused on voter registration and mobilization in an effort to defeat the Republicans. Their efforts and strategy paid off. With the unified support of the black community, my father included, Johnson won the election by a large margin.

Nineteen sixty-five wasn't the year I learned to understand my father, but it was the year I began to question his politics and challenge his stands. After all, he had taught me to not fear dissent and to welcome opposing opinions.

It took me a while, but finally secure in my position, I phoned my cousin Chuckie back with the real scoop: "Dad says he's Independent!" Yes, he was.

7

Living Up to the Legend

Jackie and I had a special bond from the beginning. While I adored my baby brother, my relationship with David would develop more in our adult years. My two brothers were a study in contrasts. David was self-reliant, easy to please, adventuresome, and funny. Jackie was far more complicated. He was rebellious yet sensitive, straightforward and passionate yet shut off, quiet at times and at other times rambunctious. When Jackie misbehaved, I loved him. When he was sweet, quiet, thoughtful, and warm, I adored him.

At times, I felt sorry for my big brother. As a teenager, he frequently stayed out past his curfew. I would wait up in my bed listening for the sound of the car on the pebbles in the driveway. The moment I heard the front door close and knew that he was safe, I would cover my ears with a pillow hoping not to hear my father's angry voice.

Other times, I'd be so angry with him he would have to hold me back from striking him. Through it all, we loved each other deeply.

The complexity of Jackie's personality and behavior had its roots in the fact that he was born November 18, 1946, and then named Jack Roosevelt Robinson Jr. When he was born, Dad had just completed his highly acclaimed inaugural season in Canada and was about to begin his first season with the Brooklyn Dodgers. When my dad took the field for his first time in Dodger blue, Mom took Jackie with her to Ebbets field. Jackie was thrown into the noble experiment right alongside our parents, and because of his name, there was no hiding place.

As a toddler, Jackie was treated like the littlest prince in major league baseball. He captured the attention of the other ballplayers, the often overzealous fans, and the media. Cameramen wanted him to pose, kids wanted to play with Jackie Robinson's son, women felt it was their right to grab him and hug him tight. He was given gifts wherever he went: lollipops at the drugstore, bologna at the butcher, potato chips at the grocery store, and cookies at the bakery.

Once, when Jackie was about three, he was visiting the ballpark during an exhibition game. Apparently, he slipped unnoticed onto the playing field and started performing. The fans were delighted. They threw money from the stands and even approached him for autographs. Another time, a member of the Dodger organization put a regulation-size bat into Jackie's small hands expecting him to be able to hit the ball. After several attempts, Jackie threw the bat down in frustration.

At times, the pressure associated with Dad's fame was obviously beyond Jackie's ability to cope. The strain first started to show when he was four and Dad took him to the rodeo. It was a rare father-son excursion and Jackie, who was heavy into his cowboy phase, was promised a special day. When Dad and Jackie arrived, the promoters made a big fuss over their presence, in spite of my father's appeal not to have too much attention drawn to him. The fans mobbed Dad, asked for his autograph, stared from a distance, teased Jackie, waved, and shouted Dad's name. The situation quickly got out of hand. Dad, fearing that Jackie might get crushed, hoisted him onto his shoulders and fled the

stadium. Jackie arrived home still shaking. He had also lost his
new cap.

After that traumatic day, Jackie got increasingly sensitive
toward strangers. Once, he shouted at a strange woman about to
pounce, "Go 'way, I hate people!" At two Jackie loved to pose for
photographers; by three he became very defensive of his personal
space. When *Life* sent a film crew to our house to get family
photos for a cover story, Jackie kept his back to the cameras. *Life*
ran the photo with my parents poised graciously on their front
steps. At their feet, Jackie Junior sat on his tricycle, his arms
folded defiantly across his chest, his head held high, and his face
obscured.

Jackie did attempt to play Little League Babe Ruth baseball, but
when the other fathers constantly compared him to his father, he
quit. From that point on, he confined his ball playing to our neighborhood games. Jackie was stocky, strong, muscular, and extremely
well coordinated, but he refused to play sports in high school.

Unable to shield my brothers and me from the outside pressures,
my parents' tendency was to overprotect and overindulge. At home
voices were rarely raised, spankings not used for punishment, and
cursing considered inappropriate. While David and I preferred our
independence and were self-disciplined, Jackie was more dependent, pampered, and needy. The women of the household, my
mother, grandmother, Willette, and me, as if to compensate for his
perceived vulnerability, ran around anticipating Jackie's needs
before he had time to express them. Jackie's school clothes were
ironed and neatly placed on his spare bed. He didn't need an alarm
clock, he was gently roused each morning even if it took several
attempts. If Jackie missed the school bus (which he often did), he
could count on Mom driving him to school. Jackie didn't have to
clean his room, take out the trash, or feed the dog, and as he got
older, he was even dismissed from Saturday-morning gardening. In
contrast, Dad would only call David once to get up and help cut
the grass; if he did not respond, Dad headed out to do the work
and at the first sound of the tractor engine, David was out of bed
and outside, ready to assist our father.

Mom can still recall the stares and whispers when she took Jackie to school on his first day. But it was what happened inside the building that was most detrimental. While my parents and the teachers recognized early that Jackie either had a learning disability or an emotional blockage interfering with his learning, they didn't know how to remedy the situation. By the second grade, he was reading below his grade level. As could have been predicted, Jackie fell further and further behind. Teachers complained constantly that he didn't complete homework assignments, had a short attention span, and was disruptive in the classroom. By the time he left elementary school, the stage was set for repeated school failures.

Some of Jackie's behavior seemed like typical boy behavior and was accepted as such. Other times it was excessive. When I was three, Jackie, then five, sent me behind a neighbor's garage under some false pretense, and purportedly neglected to warn me about the beehive. I ran out screaming and covered with bees. At times, he would hold me down and tickle me until I cried. Despite all this, I easily fell into the role of my brother's protector. When Jackie was little, he feared the dark and would call for me to turn on the bathroom light. Unable to reach the light switch, I would drag a chair to the wall, turn on the light, then return to my own bed. A few years later, in spite of my mother's warnings to the contrary, I was running up and down the hill in our backyard fetching water and food for my brothers while they sat on the bank of the lake fishing.

Accustomed to being pampered, Jackie seemed the least able to handle his frustrations. It showed up most clearly when he went to school. Because he had difficulties with reading and completing homework and was disruptive in class, teachers constantly sent home complaints. Yet Jackie was inwardly and outwardly challenged to compete with a father who was revered by the world. Feeling inadequate, he seemed to ascribe to the theory that by acting out he could become the center of attention without meeting the demands of real achievement. It worked.

Jackie's propensity to disrupt contrasted with David's ability to make the family laugh. It seemed just as easy for David to screw his face into one of his goofy expressions as it was for Jackie to seduce us into believing one of his tall tales. I think it was Jackie's big eyes, with those long eyelashes and bushy eyebrows, that made him so irresistible. I was sure that it was David's deep dimples and laughing eyes that added to his charm. My brothers were quite a pair and I was usually willing to go along with their games.

Once, when our parents were out of town and we were left behind with our least favorite baby-sitter, Mrs. Johnson, Jackie came up with a plan to get rid of her. Before my parents left, my brothers and I overheard her assuring Mom and Dad that she could manage the three of us just fine. Exchanging mischievous smiles, we met secretly in Jackie's room later that night and listened to Jackie's strategy for rebellion.

It was clear from Jackie's tone that, despite her size, this three-hundred-pound woman did not have a chance. While the first two days were tense, they did not come close to the chaos of the third day. Jackie had gotten on Mrs. Johnson's last nerve.

If I had to pinpoint her most odious quality, I would say that it was the fact that she couldn't cook and we were used to the best. When Mrs. Johnson called us to dinner on that third night, I could see the determination on Jackie's face. He took his plate and poured the food, which we were sure she got out of a can, into the garbage. This gesture wasn't enough apparently, and Jackie added insult to injury by calling Mrs. Johnson "fat." Sensing that he had gone too far, he took off, running at top speed, down the hallway, dodging in and out of rooms. Mrs. Johnson was hot on his trail. The whole scene would have been comical if it had not been for the fact that Mrs. Johnson was carrying a sixty-four-ounce, unopened can of Hawaiian Punch. The can was poised, ready to toss at her target, which, in this case, was our brother. David and I watched—speechless.

Jackie darted into his room for the second time, knowing that the passage from his bedroom through the bathroom and into David's room was too narrow for the obese woman. Just as he reached the bathroom door and turned into the tiny room, Mrs.

Johnson hurled the can. It crashed against the wall, thankfully missing its target, but leaving a gash in the wall. My eyes nearly jumped
out of my head. Oh, what is my mother going to say now, I
thought.

When our parents called that evening, Jackie tried to beat Mrs.
Johnson to the phone so he could tell his side of the story first.
David and I, trying to maintain some distance, lay on the floor near
our big brother, watching and listening to every "But, Mom!"

Well, that little incident got our mother home real quick. With
a gleam in our eyes, we pointed out the dent created in the wall
by the can of juice. This was our evidence against Mrs. Johnson.
She was fired immediately. Jackie was grounded.

In spite of Jackie's tendency to get into trouble, he was still the
oldest and I looked up to him. I remember my first crush on a boy.
Since there were few black boys in my visual scope, I, naturally,
became attracted to the one who spent time in our house, Bradley
Gordon. While Jackie and Bradley had a good laugh over that and
teased me with no mercy, they also tried to preserve my dignity by
not telling everyone about my crush. There were times that I could
go to my big brother Jackie and get sound advice. As I got older and
would attempt to describe an interesting boy, I could not get away
with saying that he was nice. Jackie reminded me that anyone can
act nice on the surface but that I should look to the character under-
neath. I would have to come up with other descriptions to meet
Jackie's critical appraisal.

Of the three of us, my older brother was the undisputed ring-
leader, and to compensate for some of the smallness Jackie felt
when comparing himself to Dad, he declared himself "king" of the
game room. Jackie would grant his subjects (David and me)
entrance into his domain only with promises of milk shakes. We
didn't care. It was fun serving our big brother from behind the
built-in ice cream soda fountain. We took turns playing soda fountain tender, passing the tall glasses of vanilla shakes across the
turquoise-laminated countertop to the eager customers perched
upon matching vinyl-covered bar stools on the other side.

Jackie carefully instructed David and me on the proper handling

of the pool cues but gave away few of his winning strategies. His
intention was to protect the tightly stretched green felt cover and
not to arm the competition. He declared the pool table off limits
to David and me when he was not around, and if we dared to defy
our older brother's mandate and play pool in his absence, we did
so fully aware that detection could result in bodily harm.

Ironically, even Jackie's power with the pool cue was eroded by
the mere fact that in order to get to the game room you had to
pass through a room devoted to our father's achievements. It was
like a shrine which sent us through an emotional gauntlet where
everything reminded us of our father's prowess, his celebrity, his
godlike stature. There were plaques, trophies, and prized baseball
memorabilia encased in glass. I couldn't read all the citations. It
would have taken hours. But I had my favorites. Dad's size-thirteen
football shoe that had been bronzed and affixed to a wooden base
at a forty-five-degree angle. The sterling silver Louisville Slugger
with his signature engraved in the middle. The photograph of him
sliding into home plate with his right arm in the air, hand
clenched victoriously in a fist, face reflecting his fierce determination. The words "brotherhood" . . . "humanitarian" . . . "distinguished" . . . "justice" . . . were all inscribed on the plaques. Words
that described deeds and attributes that went beyond baseball.

This trophy room was a tribute to one man's glory, but it was
also vexing, a source of anxiety. As I grew older, and my feelings
toward my father grew more complex, my attitude toward his
accomplishments did as well. Outwardly, my brothers and I presented a nonchalant attitude about it. But inside, each new plaque,
trophy, or key to the city ate a deeper hole in my stomach. I can
only imagine their impact on my brothers.

Looking back, I can see that Dad's bigger-than-life stature and
my mother's perfection played havoc with our developing adoles-
cence and self-esteem. Jackie, David, and I were just average kids—
we brought home report cards with more C's than D's; we were
good athletes, but not outstanding. We were well trained, polite,
friendly, and aware of the world beyond us. There was, however,
nothing in our lives that gave us the sense that we would excel as

our father had. In fact, there was much evidence to the contrary. As childhood faded, the pressure to achieve escalated. The question was in what area and by what criteria should we measure our own success?

For Jackie, this question was virtually impossible to answer, so he fled from the source of anxiety. At age sixteen, he ran away from home and headed to California. Looking back, it shouldn't have been a surprise. From repeated school absences, conferences with the principal over truancy, changing school environments in search of the right fit, he'd been trying to escape for a long time. The fact that Jackie hadn't even shared his plans with David or me was symptomatic of the isolation and alienation he probably felt even within our family. No one knew where he was until after a few days on his own, struck by the reality of what he had done, Jackie returned home. But years would go by before he truly "came home." At seventeen, Jackie finally gave up on school, and maybe himself. He dropped out of high school and joined the Army.

Jackie's first duty was at Fort Riley, Kansas. Even the Army couldn't contain his discontent. After checking out the social life on base, Jackie found out that because of his age he couldn't get into the military clubs or bars where most of the entertainment took place. Bored, lost, and troubled, he filled his time smoking marijuana and popping pills. In this frame of mind, four months after he was inducted into the Army, Jackie was shipped to Vietnam, arriving in Cam Ranh Bay in July of 1964. Jackie Junior was immediately struck by the fact that Vietnam was a study in contrasts. The rich, beautiful, forested country; the devastation caused by war. A member of the 1st Infantry Battalion, he experienced no military action for the first couple of months, so while he had joined the Army looking for discipline and a sense of purpose, he found instead boredom, underutilization, and terror. To make matters worse, he was involved in a poorly understood war, and his letters revealed his frustrations with the conflicting attitudes of the United States government and the people back home.

Home. That in itself was confusing for my brother. Jackie was sent to fight a war during a time when racial tensions in his coun-

try had reached a peak. And he had received a letter from his girlfriend, Penny, telling him that she was pregnant. Jackie wrote me
about Penny's pregnancy and asked me to help break the news to
Mom and Dad.

My parents, knowing that Jackie would not take full responsibility for the child he helped create, were shaken and angry, but
since he was in Vietnam, they could not express their feelings
except through the mail. Penny's father must have also been feeling the frustration of not being able to get to Jackie directly, so he
called our house and threatened my brother through us. I was the
one at home to receive that call. I took his angry words literally
and was shaken by the seriousness of his threat. The entire situation confused me, since I felt joyous at the prospect of a niece or
nephew. By the time my brother's daughter, Sonya, was born, attitudes had softened. But true to my parents fears, my brother, even
when he returned from Vietnam, was in no shape to parent.

I learned much later the reasons why. During the remainder of
Jackie's time in Vietnam, he had seen quite a few combat missions
and witnessed the blurring of the enemy lines. The South
Vietnamese farmers, women, and children became suspected of
hiding the enemy within their villages. The American soldiers were
accused of killing indiscriminately. The North Vietnamese receded
into the countryside to fight a guerrilla war of ambush, mines, and
booby traps. Casualties were high. Meanwhile, the Black GIs
accused the white officers of racism, saying that they spent a dis-
proportionate amount of time on the front line.

To ease the frustrations and calm their fears, marijuana, heroin,
and opium were used as combat-zone coping devices, replacing
alcohol as the drug of choice in previous wars. In Vietnam, marijuana grew in the wild and was smoked in its pure form, dipped
in opium, a plant indigenous to Southeast Asia.

Jackie's tour of duty ended abruptly after he was hit with
shrapnel that killed the men on either side of him. The Army sent
him home with a small black box containing a Purple Heart and
a sizable drug addiction. Jackie stepped off the plane and passed
unnoticed through Army Inspection with his own mementos

from the war, a duffel bag with eighty opium-treated marijuana cigarettes.

Initially, Jackie stayed at home but avoided speaking about the combat he had seen. Instead, he talked about the Vietnamese people who impressed him with their resourcefulness and survival instincts. It was obvious that he was anxious and distraught. What was less obvious to us right away was the seriousness of his drug habit.

My family delighted in Jackie's return home, thinking that he would be more mature, with goals and a plan for his future. We quickly discovered that Jackie had changed, but not for the better. In fact, his return signaled the beginning of repeated crises that would tear at the fibers of what was once a close-knit family.

As if in anticipation of a fierce hurricane, each of us sought a space called "survival" in our own way, happiness on our own terms. Mom plunged more seriously into her career, not foreseeing the opposition she would soon receive at home. Dad moved with deliberate speed and unpredictability through the world of politics and business. He started several unsuccessful businesses, co-founded Freedom National Bank in Harlem, and struggled with his diabetes. His hair had grayed. He was overweight. And he appeared to have aged far beyond his forty-four years. David was about to graduate from New Canaan Country Day School and trade the serenity of the woods surrounding our property for uncharted adventures in boarding school. And I buried myself in romance and intrigue, boys and partying.

Jackie, oblivious to what was happening in anyone's life but his own, took off for Colorado Springs in his red convertible with his buddy, Issac Parham. They were both in need of money to support drug habits and knew that they could make some money with cards. Issac, who had practically learned to count on dice, was a master with a deck of cards, and was an obvious choice for Jackie's traveling partner.

A throwback to the Wild West, in Colorado Springs carrying weapons openly was legal and gambling a part of life. Once they arrived in Colorado Springs, Issac played cards and won, and Jackie watched his back. The twosome quickly got a reputation, which included talk of their cheating. And while Jackie and Issac considered themselves invincible, even they knew when it was time to leave town. After a very lucrative first trip, they returned to the East Coast.

Caught between the allure of two worlds, the street life which offered him anonymity and the one connected to our father, which promised only disappointment, Jackie chose not to stay at home. Instead he lived in hotels in and about Stamford. Meanwhile, Mom, Dad, and I lived with conjecture over my brother's whereabouts but with no definitive clues. The less we saw of him, the more we worried. The not knowing combined with our own suspicions kept us always ready for news of a major disaster. Each evening Dad greeted me with: "Any word from Jackie?"

8

Love and War

While Jackie's life seemed to be spinning out of control, mine, on the surface at least, seemed hopelessly conventional. I was fifteen and entering my junior year in high school, and my steady boyfriend, Lenny, and I planned to get married when I graduated from college. In the meantime though, he joined the Army, and when he left for the Texas base he'd been assigned to, I vowed not to go out with anyone else.

I knew living up to that commitment wouldn't be easy. It was such an extreme promise I had to take drastic measures to keep it, the first being to drop out of the party scene. And, so that I wouldn't miss going to parties, I took up knitting.

That kept my hands and mind occupied for a while at least. Knitting was a passion I shared with my maternal grandmother, an expert who could juggle three or four projects at a time.

"Grandma, I want to make Lenny a sweater," I told her one afternoon.

"I'm in the middle of making your mother a mohair dress," she answered. "I'd welcome the company."

She picked me up at school the next afternoon and took me to her favorite knitting shop. We found a pattern for a man's crew neck sweater—no cables, a simple alternating knit-pearl design. I nearly got lost in the huge selection of yarn. A row of blue/green fibers caught my eye. The colors would look good next to Lenny's chocolate brown skin, a peaceful combination, easy on the eyes. Satisfied with my choice, I counted out the correct number of skeins, while Grandma suggested that I use size-twelve knitting needles: "The larger needle will help you move the project along more quickly."

That sounded good to me; there was little time to spare. I was determined to give Lenny the sweater for Christmas.

Grandma and I lost no time in getting right to work when we returned. I cast on sixty-two stitches and completed the three-inch ribbing for the back of the sweater before I went to bed that first night.

Thereafter, Grandma assumed the role of Sweater Project Consultant, interpreting the pattern as we went along. She put my feet to the flame of perfection, and if I tried to ignore a dropped stitch, she would make me tear out rows until I got back to it, picked it up, and knitted the whole section over again.

I worked on the sweater every afternoon for the next six weeks. I would come home from school, grab a snack, and join Grandma in her bedroom just as the music swelled for her favorite soap opera, "The Doctors."

This was not for mere entertainment. Grandma had a plan. While she had my attention, she decided to use the time to hammer home her message: I should enter the medical profession. Grandma was far too traditional to suggest that I shoot for medical school. She was clear on that point: The profession of nursing was more suitable for women, medicine for men. While she held nursing in the highest esteem, she also believed that the ultimate goal for any sharp, attractive nurse was to marry a doctor. In case I got confused about this, "The Doctors" was there to reinforce the message.

Grandma didn't stop there. Subtle messages were strewn all around, like the paperback doctor/nurse romance novels she stored in her bedside tables. These thin, easy-to-read books all had sexy covers, piquing my adolescent curiosity. I wanted to experience similar passion. Feel the heat. Not exactly what was going on in my relationship with Lenny, who felt more like a big brother than my ideal lover. The passion I felt toward him certainly paled in comparison to the lusty entanglements all those doctors and nurses were getting mixed up in.

By the time I was sixteen, I had read most of the books. This was no easy task. Since I hadn't actually asked Grandma for permission, I had to sneak the books out of her room, read the lurid passages in the privacy of my bedroom, and then replace them, hoping they hadn't been missed.

I wasn't really worried about my grandmother discovering my secret. I felt sure that she *knew* I was reading them, and that she *wanted* me to read them, hoping that they would add the necessary spice to her plan that I marry a doctor. Grandma was well aware of my stubbornness and was careful not to push her opinion upon me, particularly when it mattered most. She knew that if she came out and told me what to do, the likelihood was I'd do just the opposite.

I still remember her disappointment when I refused to participate in her club's spring cotillion. Considering how much I loved to go to parties, Grandma was correct to think that I would be tempted by the cotillion. On the surface, it was nothing more than a grand party. She tried a quiet sell approach with cautious optimism: the romantic evening, a full-length gown, waltzing with a handsome escort, the before and after parties, my name in the newspaper. I wouldn't budge. The cotillion, a turning point for the upper-class girl, signaling her preparation for high society, was economically out of reach for the average black family, and I wanted no part of the whole scene. One of the frivolities of the elite, I thought. When I stood my ground, Grandma tried to elicit support from Mom and Dad. Since they did not have strong feelings either way, they left the decision up to me.

I was appreciative of the fact that my parents had not placed class restrictions on my friendships or preached any stereotypes associated with one group of people over another. Instead, they reinforced values: education, service, achievement, family. Their only restriction was a ban on public dances. Even their insistence on our membership in Jack & Jill was not about class so much as an attempt to balance the whiteness of our home and school environments. As the deadline for cotillion recommendations encroached, my grandmother made one final attempt to sway me. Again, I declined.

Defeated, Grandma let the issue of the cotillion drop. She concentrated instead on convincing me to marry the right man. This was problematic. In spite of the indoctrination I received from my grandmother, the boys I had so far expressed interest in were definitely not heading for medical school.

As our project neared completion, my grandmother anticipated the loss of our quality time together. She decided to up the ante, and became more serious about the issue of marriage. One afternoon, as our fingers worked furiously with the rhythmic click of the knitting needles, Grandma cleared her throat:

"You know, Sharon, I was married twice."

"Yeah, Uncle Chuck's father, right?" I replied without taking my eyes off my knitting. Grandma rarely talked about her first husband, but I sensed that she wanted to now. "Tell me about him?"

Grandma did: "His name was Charles Williams. We met when I was a teenager in Nogales, Arizona. I was working in my father's restaurant. Charles was a soldier stationed in a nearby fort. He used to come to the restaurant looking so handsome in his uniform that I couldn't stop looking at him," she said, shaking her head in an approving way.

"Arizona?" I hadn't known there were black people in the Southwest. "How did your family end up in Arizona?"

"My father was a chef on the railroad. His cooking was so popular that the president of Mexico asked him to come work on his private car. When he got down to Mexico he opened up two restaurants in Guadalajara. That lasted until the Mexican govern-

ment nationalized the country and made all the Americans get
out. My father landed in Nogales, where he opened a restaurant
and later a movie theater."

"Were there any black people there?" I was still trying to picture this apparently pioneering black man.

"Well, yes, there were the soldiers stationed in Nogales and their
families. Anyway, Charles stood maybe six feet tall. He was light-
skinned and had good hair." I knew what she meant. "All the girls
were after him but he chose me. I was so happy when he proposed.
My mother didn't approve of us getting married, so we eloped.
Turns out she was right because our marriage didn't last long. As
soon as Charles received his discharge papers, he went back home
to Chicago, leaving me pregnant with your uncle Chuck. I never
saw him again."

Grandma sat quietly as she finished her story, only her hands still
busy knitting the gold mohair.

"I was too proud to cry much. Couldn't let your great-grandmother know how hurt I was."

I didn't say anything. I felt sad for my grandmother and understood why I had heard so little about my uncle Chuck's father.

"Lenny's a nice boy and all, Sharon. But you're too young to
know true love. Be careful."

She stopped, not wanting to lecture me. She reached for my
knitting and said, "Let me see that panel." The back measured
about twelve inches now and I could see my progress. I was also
thankful that Grandma had dropped the subject of marriage.

The four-piece sweater puzzle was finally completed and
Grandma took the sections to a seamstress who sewed them
together, blocked the sweater, and returned it to us looking as if it
had been professionally made. I couldn't believe that I had made it
and wondered what Lenny would say.

He arrived home a few days before Christmas. I presented him
with the sweater the moment he walked through the door. My
eyes did not leave his face: first a grin, then, a broad smile. Lenny
slipped the sweater over his head. It looked as if he'd gone to
Bloomingdale's and tried on sweaters until he found the perfect fit.

He wrapped his strong arms around me, nearly smothering me with his tight grip. "Thank you. I love it," he whispered in my ear as he bent to kiss me.

While Lenny was home on leave we saw each other daily. He told me he was going to be away for a year or more at Officers' Training School and then he would probably be sent to Vietnam. Lenny had a gentle soul and I wondered what the war would do to him. I knew what it had done to my brother. The possibility of losing him brought us even closer both emotionally and physically. The decision to have sex came after hours of discussion and was fueled more by fear than passion. I felt good about the decision though—after all, we loved each other. So, the weekend before he left, we consummated our relationship. I remember wondering afterward if my parents would be able to tell just by looking at me. So I felt a little guilty, too. But Lenny and I parted with promises of fidelity and everlasting love.

Within a week of Lenny's departure, my friends Candy, Wendy Wise, and Linda Dubissette descended upon me. Determined not to let me slip back into isolation, or knitting, they began plotting to get me back into partying. I was torn. A year was a long time. I wasn't really ready to commit to staying at home for the remainder of my high school years. Yet I feared partying would lead to dating and an eventual breakup with Lenny. I didn't want that.

I decided to talk with Jackie and let him play big brother. We had barely spoken to each other since his return from Vietnam, and I didn't know what his advice would be—still, I wanted it.

Jackie, as it turned out, approached me first.

"Sharon," Jackie said, standing in my bedroom doorway one evening. "Word on the street is that you and Lenny are tight. What's the story?"

"He just left to go to Texas for Officers' Training School. Then he goes to Vietnam," I replied, searching my brother's eyes for a response to my mention of the war.

"I hope you broke up with him," Jackie stated without emotion.

"No, I promised to wait for him."

"I suppose he said he'd wait for you, too," Jackie said. "Forget him, Sharon. I've been there. He'll have a girlfriend on base and one in town by next week."

I didn't want to believe my brother, and I protested, shaken by what he was saying: "Jackie, you don't understand. I plan to marry Lenny someday. I promised him that I'd wait."

"You're too young to think about marrying anyone, especially a man who's off to war. Go out with your friends and have fun," he insisted.

I was saddened by the finality of his words. I knew that he was speaking from experience. Jackie was usually straight with me. Sometimes his blunt honesty and relentless teasing would set me off. This particular discussion had been calm, thoughtful, open— hard to dismiss. But I also believed that Lenny would be counting on coming home to me. "I'll think about it."

Eventually, I picked up the phone and called Linda.

"I just had a talk with Jackie. Even he thinks that I need to go out. You still want to go to that party next weekend?"

Linda had moved from North Carolina the previous year. Her father was one of two black physicians in town. She was an attractive girl with straight hair and light eyes, and a Southern accent we weren't accustomed to hearing. The boys were all over her.

We became fast friends. She loved to party and was as into boys as I was; school was secondary in our lives. I had slightly more career ambition than Linda, who had no idea what she wanted to be, but what we talked about incessantly was boys and sex. What we didn't know we looked up in her father's medical books. What they didn't reveal we found in the library.

Linda and I had dated guys who were older than us by a couple of years, guys with far more experience and street smarts, because we liked the contrast. Fear of pregnancy kept us virgins our first year of high school.

The party I agreed to go to with Linda was the opening of a new club for teenagers in downtown Stamford. Linda sweetened the pot by saying that she had heard that boys from the Norwalk High basketball team were coming over. Mom even cooperated and made an exception to the public dance rule. She had not liked me giving up my social life and was happy to see me rejoin my friends.

We arrived at the club just as the party atmosphere was beginning to move into full swing and began to cruise the room with an exaggerated air of confidence. Linda, spotting the group from Norwalk, steered us toward them. There were two particularly striking young men in the group of five or so that I recognized from Norwalk High basketball games. Their laughter stopped dead as they watched us approach. They greeted Linda, and she made the introductions: Calvin Murphy, LaSalle Reynolds, and Michael Williams. Their names were familiar. I nodded to Calvin and LaSalle but my gaze stayed on Michael. The other two men volunteered their names, but I wasn't paying attention.

The attraction was immediate. Michael returned my stare with equal intensity. Once our eyes met and locked, I was held captive by the warmth of his smile. It reminded me of my father's. Michael stood six feet, but because of his broad, muscular shoulders he appeared much larger. He was clean-shaven, and I felt the urge to rub my hand on his face to see if it was as smooth as it looked. Michael held my hand for what seemed like an eternity and spoke with a deep, passionate voice. I was a little embarrassed, but then he asked me to dance.

One dance with Michael flowed into five. Except for the transition in our dance tempo, we barely noticed the change in tunes. We talked easily, as if we were old friends. Michael was a senior at Norwalk High School, one of nine children, his father worked for the city and his mother was a housewife. He was a local basketball hero with NBA ambitions . . . and he was very handsome.

Michael seemed the master of charm and sophistication, mixed with warmth and attentiveness. The intensity of my feelings for him struck a chord—it reminded me of the passion described in my grandmother's romance books. When Linda came to tell me that her father was outside, I suddenly resented our curfew, but tried not to let it show. Michael walked me to the door and we said good night, confident that this was only a beginning. He promised to call me.

I sat quietly in the backseat of Linda's father's car listening to the whispering that went on between Wendy and Candy. Candy liked LaSalle. Wendy hadn't met anyone new. I could tell from their conversation that they'd had a good time, but it couldn't compare to the magic of mine.

Wendy slept over my house that night. She talked in fast forward. "Did you see the way Michael looked at you? Girl, do you know he's a basketball star? I saw him play once. Kept getting those rebounds. And is he ever handsome. Girl, you need to forget Lenny. I mean he's nice and all but Michael is *fine*."

I thought of my grandmother's warnings and wondered if he'd be a heartbreaker.

At least I didn't have to say a word. Wendy was content to talk to herself if necessary. I lay in my bed replaying the evening. Thinking about his hands. His broad shoulders. How firmly he'd grasped my hand. How sweetly he'd kissed me on the cheek, promising to call. Yeah, I had to admit—he was smooth. I felt disloyal to Lenny, and confused by this rapid onset of feelings for another guy. But what I had felt for Lenny didn't begin to compare to this.

"You should have seen the two of you on the dance floor. You didn't miss a beat. The perfect couple. Girl, I know this is the real thing. I'm so happy for you. Don't you feel anything? Talk to me. You've got to feel lucky, happy, interested, something. I saw you two out there. It was as if you knew each other for years. "

I smiled, thinking this girl is not going to let me get any sleep tonight unless I tell her something.

"I'll write Lenny in the morning. Tell him I'm going to date other people. I hope Michael calls. You never know about these things. So, don't go getting us married so quickly." I was lying through my teeth. I was gone, already fantasizing about the beautiful children we would have together. Lenny would have to understand. He was a practical sort of guy. He would want the best for me.

But I tossed in my canopy bed, Lenny's image in my mind. I hated to hurt him. What could I say in my letter? Hadn't I just made a promise to wait for him? Now he'd be going off to war with a broken heart. Maybe I'm exaggerating, I thought. Who knows how he'll really feel? He may already have a girlfriend on the base, as Jackie had suggested. He probably wasn't being faithful either. He might even be relieved. I knew that I was stretching, trying to rationalize what I planned to do.

I lay in bed, thinking of all the messages that I had received lately: Jackie's advice, Wendy's excitement, Michael's charm, Lenny's promise. I arose the next morning worn out. After Mom and I took Wendy home, I headed straight to my desk. I wrote Lenny a short "Dear John" note. I never heard from him again.

Within a few months from the day we met, Michael and I were a hot new item, the envy of all our friends. Not a day went by without at least one telephone conversation. We talked long into the night.

Most of our weekends were reserved for Norwalk High basketball games and parties. Candy and I sat in the bleachers at as many of Norwalk's games as we could. She was dating Michael's friend LaSalle, who maintained a rebounding average close to Michael's. We shouted louder for numbers 32 (Michael) and 43 (LaSalle) than anyone surrounding us, in the hopes that our men would feel as if they were stars.

With Michael, Calvin, and LaSalle in their senior year, it was their last attempt to win the Fairfield County Interscholastic Athletic Conference (CIAC) Class A Basketball Tourney semifinals. Calvin, the team's captain, lead the state and New England in scoring, averaging forty points per game. The press described him as "brilliant," "sensational," and "the master magician" of basketball. His nosebleeds and a case of tonsillitis made headlines. One afternoon, a bunch of us were at the playground watching the guys show off on the basketball court. To our amazement, five-foot-ten-inch Calvin dunked the ball, resting his elbows on the basketball hoop. We went wild.

While the press credited Michael with being a steady performer, averaging ten points per game, and a great rebounder, there was only one star on the team. Michael played in Calvin's shadow for three years.

That season Norwalk won twenty-three of twenty-four games, including four in the tourney, and won its first championship. Calvin and Michael were selected for the CIAC L Division All-Tournament team by the local sportswriters. It was one of those moments when life was perfect.

Moments, by definition, pass. Not long after the basketball season ended, Calvin accepted a four-year scholarship to Niagara University. Up to that point a number of colleges had been courting Calvin and Michael, hoping to get them as a package deal. But once Calvin decided to go to Niagara, the wooing of Michael ended. No college offered Michael a basketball scholarship.

The rejections hurt and embittered Michael. He had given his best to the game of basketball and neglected his studies, all the while believing that his athlete status would somehow protect him. Not a new story, perhaps, and one still being replayed endlessly. But the problem was that as his disappointment, frustration, and anger grew, Michael turned them on me.

I wasn't sure at first why Michael insisted that I wear my skirts below my knees, because the fashion ultimate was the mini-skirt. But I willingly complied, believing he just didn't want anyone looking at his lady. He bragged to his sisters that I didn't smoke, drink alcohol, or curse. I felt uncomfortable up on that pedestal, but I pushed my concerns to the back of my mind, supposing that this was Michael's way of demonstrating his pride in me.

Meanwhile, he was solicitous, gentle, and reliable. We kissed and touched each other with urgency and love. Petting just short of intercourse seemed to satisfy Michael as much as it did me. I was relieved that he didn't pressure me for sex. I knew the question was inevitable, but wanted to postpone it for as long as possible.

In the hallways of Stamford High, the locker talk was all about sex. We kept count of which girls had succumbed to their boyfriends' pressure. Even though I had lost my virginity to Lenny earlier that year, I wasn't ready to have sex with Michael. We hadn't been dating that long. Besides, I told myself, I might really marry this man. Since he was a senior, and I a junior, we could conceivably get married after I graduated. I wanted to save our lovemaking until after we married.

To my dismay, my fairy-tale romance with Michael ended abruptly. I picked up the phone one day and heard a voice I was not familiar with. Gone was the warm, loving tone. It was replaced by a cold, flat voice. I was startled. I knew immediately that something was drastically wrong.

"What's the matter?" I asked, genuinely concerned.

"Did you have sex with Lenny?" He spoke curtly into the phone.

"Yes, Michael," I replied, insulted by his tone and wanting to say, "Is that all?" I thought someone had died. I had never asked him if he had had sex with his old girlfriends. I assumed that he had.

"Where were you?" he demanded.

"What difference does that make?" I replied stubbornly, though I didn't feel as if I had anything to hide. Lenny and I had been in love. We had been together for over a year before deciding to have sex. I wasn't about to start defending that decision. "Look, Michael, I don't want to discuss this any further. What do you want to do this weekend?" I said, trying to change the subject.

"I'll pick you up Friday at eight, we can decide then." He slammed the phone down without saying good-bye. Initially, I was annoyed, but as the night wore on and Michael did not call back and apologize, guilt set in. For the first time, I regretted my decision to have sex with Lenny.

The next night Michael didn't call me and I refused to call him. I wanted to give him some time, hoping it would erase the bad feeling that had come over him. Friday, I dressed for our date with apprehension, sensing that the subject was not dead. Michael arrived on time, driving his father's station wagon. He was polite while in the house, yet distant. He opened the passenger door of his car and I climbed in. Suddenly, I felt submissive, like a guilty child.

"Where are we going?" I asked, hopeful that the response would be positive.

"We're going to talk some more," he responded gruffly. I sighed but didn't protest. I could tell he was mad, hurt. In a way, maybe someone had died: the perfect girlfriend Michael had assumed me to be.

Michael drove to a dark, often deserted street bordering on the reservoir. We called the street Lovers' Lane because kids often parked there to neck. I shifted in my seat, unnerved by the tense silence. Michael drummed on the dashboard, not looking at me.

"You didn't answer my question the other night. Where did you and Lenny go the night you had sex? Were you in his car? In his house?"

"We went over to a friend's apartment," I answered, somewhat disturbed that I had fallen into his trap.

"Did you have any clothes on?" he asked, almost without emotion.

I was beginning to feel scared. I didn't want to answer that question. His curiosity didn't seem normal, and it certainly wasn't any of his business. Yet the tension frightened me. I was beginning to understand that Michael felt personally violated by the fact that I was not a virgin. I was not the woman he thought he fell in love with. The image he was building made me feel cheap.

"I can't answer that," I replied softly. "Michael, it doesn't matter. Let's just forget this. That was the past." I knew that I was taking a risk with his emotions, but I had to try to get through to him and save a shred of my self-respect.

Michael drummed harder on the dashboard. He still had not looked at me. I think he hated me at that moment. Hated that his image of me was tarnished. I was not the example he had held up to his sisters.

"So, you had sex once?" he went on.

"We went there two nights in a row," I answered.

"You lied to me. You told me you only had sex once." He drummed faster. I hadn't actually said how many times we had intercourse, just that it had happened.

"It wasn't exactly a lie. It was the same weekend, just before Lenny left for officers' training. We thought that he would be sent to Vietnam. We had no idea when we'd see each other again," I pleaded, hoping for redemption. I felt as if I were on trial, fighting for my dignity. Michael was judge and jury. My fate lay in his angry hands. But I knew the verdict was already in. I just wasn't sure of the punishment.

Finally he turned to face me. The warmth that I had read in his eyes the first night we met was now replaced by anger and bitterness. "You whore, slut!" he shouted into my soul.

I winced at his words, stung by their cruelty, frightened by their meaning. Was it possible? Was he right? Did that one decision change me? Make me a bad person unworthy of love?

As Michael lashed out with his words, his hand swung wildly, landing hard on my cheek. I gasped. He hit me again, this time with all deliberation. I cried out in pain, holding my cheek to decrease the sting. As the initial shock subsided, I sat speechless, too stunned, bewildered, numb, to respond. And what was my defense? Love, commitment, lust? I had never been spoken to with such hatred. Finally getting back enough strength to feel indignation, I spoke:

"Take me home," I demanded.

"My pleasure," said Michael.

I was no longer afraid. I was angry. How dare he hit me? I won't ever go out with him again, I told myself. I'll tell Jackie and he'll beat Michael up. Then I remembered that I hardly ever saw Jackie anymore, and when I did, he didn't stay around long enough to talk. I thought about my dad but quickly dismissed that idea. He didn't approve of premarital sex and I feared that telling my father the truth would diminish me in his eyes. It was my problem to deal with alone.

We pulled up into my driveway. I was about to bolt from the car when Michael grabbed my arm and held me back. He apologized. His posture had softened, his voice was quiet, his words were reassuring. He pleaded jealousy and begged forgiveness.

Michael said all the right things. I accepted his words, and forgave him. We agreed to give our relationship another try.

And that's how it begins.

I said good night and got out of the car. As I closed the front door behind me and turned off the lights, I sighed, thankful that my parents hadn't waited up for me. My face was still stinging. I decided to put ice on my cheek, hoping it wouldn't swell. I knocked on the door to my parents' room and called out to let them know that I was home. Saying good night through the closed door, I went to my room.

Lying in bed fifteen minutes later, I realized that I had grown very fond of Michael. I wanted to continue dating him. I accepted his rationalizations for his aggressive behavior. I told myself that I was partially to blame and that it wouldn't happen again. After all, I thought, I did make him angry by not taking his concerns seriously. I vowed to put more effort into the relationship.

And that's how it continues.

9

The Power Is in the Secrecy

Everybody knows how I had to walk a tightrope when it
came to watching my behavior during that first year. If one
of the Cardinals spiked me (and I got spiked plenty) I had to
ignore it. When Ben Chapman yelled a heap of unprintable racial
epithets at me from the Phillies' dugout, I had to keep my mouth
shut. When an umpire gave me a bad call, I forced myself to
grind my teeth in silence. That was torture.

Jackie Robinson

It was months before Michael raised a hand to me again. The issue
seemed to be forgotten. Our relationship continued to grow but
there were differences. The double dating was less frequent. The
compliments nonexistent. Some days were wonderful; others bear-
able. Michael continued to bring up my past and pressure me to
have sex with him. I didn't like the pressure, but reluctantly I gave
in. I thought the physical expression of love would put his doubts
to rest. I realized afterward that all it accomplished was to increase
the control Michael had over me.

Once I was totally "his," Michael became critical of every aspect
of my life, but in such a way that I wasn't aware of the impact it
was having on me. He would disapprove of "my middle-class values," as he disparagingly referred to my college talk, and gradually,
I began to disapprove of my friends who had gone off to college.
I claimed that it changed them. When we were in my parents' presence he would tell them he approved of my going to college then
turn around and tell me differently. He would ridicule our family

vacations or the fact that I shopped at Bloomingdale's, and he said instead of focusing on a career I should aspire to being a house-wife and mother. He criticized my friends and found endless flaws in my behavior. But he continued to mix the criticism in with periods of unselfish love and attention. One minute I was the most important person in his life, the next minute he was complaining.

No matter what Michael said, I valued his opinion and inter-nalized his message. Eventually, I began to distance myself from my friends and family. Candy, Wendy, and Linda protested, trying to tell me how I'd changed, but eventually they stayed at a distance. I filled my life with Michael and his family. I spent my weekends baby-sitting for his nieces and nephews, hoping that he would praise me for my adept mothering skills. I became friendly with his sisters and even made an attempt to get to know his mother.

The relationship with my family was a bit trickier. The anger that I felt toward Michael was redirected at my mother. Her work became the enemy. Without realizing that my mother's job was essential to the family's economy, I complained that it took prece-dence over the family. Mom defended her right to have a career. The fact that my mother, as a psychiatric nurse, dealt with other people's problems all day made me resent her work even more because she seemed to not be aware of how troubled I was. The irony of teenage selfishness is that I was pushing her away, yet I felt abandoned by her.

On one level I knew that my objections to my mother's work-ing were unfair. I had never complained about my father's work. It just seemed that, for a period in my life, Mom and I clashed on all the important things. I talked of marriage, ten kids, and a farm. She talked college. Mom talked Jack & Jill. I complained that the kids were all snobs. Neither of my parents liked Michael; I thought he was the one.

As months passed, the crisis grew on all levels. I stopped want-ing to go on family vacations. I gradually lost interest in sports and dropped off the girls' basketball team; I stopped attending Jack & Jill activities altogether. I couldn't remember the good times I shared with Michael, the walks on the beach, picnics, parties.

The verbal and physical attacks I began to endure became the marker of time, negating such mundane delineations as the day of the week. My world shrank until Michael was the core around which all else revolved. I went to great lengths explaining bruises, often blaming the children for whom I baby-sat. I had been a motivated student with a B+ average; I became an unmotivated drudge, barely hanging on to a C. My dreams of college were dimming, my grades merely a reflection of how I felt about myself.

I became more miserable and withdrawn. My parents complained I was spending too much time in my room, and away from the family, but they did not seem to be aware of the seriousness of my problems.

After a year with Michael, I was exhausted, beaten down, incapable of making the simplest decision. I barely recognized myself in the mirror. Work was the only thing that kept me sane. I was a part-time nursing assistant on the medical-surgical floor of St. Joseph's Hospital, where I'd been employed since the second semester of my junior year. I had wanted to work in a hospital since before age twelve. At fourteen, I had applied for a position as a Candy Striper at Stamford Hospital but my request was denied. I was devastated: It was only a volunteer job, yet I was not welcome. The hospital's discriminatory practices kept me out. On my sixteenth birthday, I got my driver's license and Social Security card within the same week, and a few weeks later, I had an after-school job at St. Joseph's.

I admired the registered nurses on my floor. They often praised my work and I felt honored carrying out even menial tasks. I was particularly close to the head nurse, an attractive young nun who ran a strict, well-organized floor, demanding that our patients be treated with skill and caring. I responded positively to the clear direction and positive reinforcement. In her floor-length white habit, Sister Angelica greatly encouraged my interest in nursing.

I told no one of Michael's abusive behavior. I began to feel as if I were on a train that was just pulling out of the station, with no clear destination. As the train speeded up, so did my life, but getting closer to nowhere that made any sense.

I couldn't ask for help. Domestic violence? Battered women's syndrome? Those were terms not commonly used until many years later. Domestic violence was a well-kept secret. Families were supposed to keep problems to themselves, exposing only the good to others. And who could I talk to even if I'd wanted to, who could I trust? My older brother was a shadow of himself. I couldn't tell my parents; I'd have had to admit I was sexually active, and I couldn't risk losing their respect or, worse yet, their love. Besides, they had enough to worry about with Jackie. So I convinced myself that the best thing to do was to keep the problem under wraps.

I grew up watching women cater to their men. Even the preparation and serving of food in my family sent me a message. The women not only cooked the meals, they stood back until the men were served before fixing themselves a plate. My brother's problems were always more important then mine. My father's work more important than my mother's. I had fallen into all the same traps, including allowing Michael to define me.

And then Michael gave me the ring.

He had talked of marriage, but even I was taken by surprise the day early in my senior year when we went looking at rings. We found a small diamond solitaire in the jewelry store, and paid a deposit. Michael proudly presented it to me on Valentine's Day. I took the ring as a hopeful sign: Michael promised that once we were married and I was his wife, he would not hit me again. We were both euphoric. I had a definition. I was going to be Mrs. Michael Williams.

My parents were outraged, disappointed, disapproving. The audacity of their sixteen-year-old proudly sporting a diamond ring. Worse yet, to be engaged to a man my parents distrusted. I had been talking marriage and babies since age twelve, and yet my mother and father assumed that I would wait until after completing college.

But for me, with Michael's offer of marriage, the pain subsided. Life would get better. I was lovable. We made plans. It didn't matter that my parents thought I was too young or that Michael lacked skills. It seemed as if half my class at Stamford High was either engaged or having babies. I wasn't pregnant. I didn't drink.

I didn't hang out late at night and worry my parents. I only wanted to marry the man that I loved. I was convinced that my parents were unreasonable, and I wore my ring with pride.

Sister Angelica was curious about my engagement and concerned about my future. I reassured her that my marriage would not interfere with my dreams of becoming a nurse. Still, she worried. With a glint in her eye, she'd say, "Maybe I can convince you to become a nun.

"Well, I think you're doing God's work by serving the sick," she said.

"But it's work that also interferes with my going to church with Michael," I told her. "He's complaining about that."

"Why don't you try taking every other Sunday off?" she offered, and that sounded good to me, since the work was holding me together and I resisted quitting. But by January, I gave in to the pressure from Michael to quit my job and I handed in my letter of resignation. I left the floor feeling disconnected from a world that had nurtured me.

While I could quit a part-time job at St. Joseph's, my plans to become a nurse kept me tied to the notion of going to college. The voice of my mother and grandmother had gotten through to me. My preoccupation with marriage was not lost to my goal of becoming a nurse.

With something to communicate about, Mom and I sat down to discuss nursing school. With a bachelor's and master's in nursing, my mother pushed me in the direction of baccalaureate education. The more she pushed, the more I leaned toward the diploma programs. Once again we were at a test of wills. The only experience I had to go on was my year at St. Joseph's Hospital where the diploma nurses arrived on the floors with more advanced skills than the recent college graduates. My goal was to be a great clinician; I didn't care about the degree.

Michael didn't help. He didn't want me to have a career at all. But he found the concept of a diploma school slightly less threatening. I began to research diploma nursing schools in New York City and decided to apply to one of them.

My initial application was followed by a visit to the school. My mother wasn't able to attend, so I asked my father to accompany me. It was actually a relief because Dad didn't share my mother's passionate opposition to the diploma program and he was delighted to be included in the process. The day of the visit parents were given an orientation while prospective students took a series of psychological tests. Neither Dad nor I gave much thought to the impact his presence would have on the school's selection process.

When Dad and I arrived, the school administrator immediately recognized him. It was New York City, after all. I apparently passed the psychological testing, but I most certainly passed the celebrity test; as Dad and I prepared to leave, the director virtually assured me admittance to the school. I smiled outwardly but inside my self-esteem took another dive.

So when I received an acceptance letter from the nursing school in March even though I hadn't completed the application process, I turned it down. While it was probably a rationalization, I decided that the acceptance was based on the school's desire to have the daughter of a famous man in attendance. But really, the problem was that the school did not accept married students and by the time the acceptance letter arrived I was determined to get married as soon as I turned eighteen.

After a brief calm, Michael entered a period of gloom. One afternoon when he picked me up from school he took me for a long drive. We argued. In his fury Michael grabbed my left hand, pulled off my engagement ring, and threw it out the car window into the woods. The engagement was off. I told him that it didn't matter, but inside I was devastated and terrified that he would go through with what he threatened.

Over the prior six months I had contemplated suicide several times. Once, Candy and I stayed up until late one night talking on the phone about ways to commit suicide. But I had never acted on my thoughts before. Arriving home from the fight with Michael, I just wanted the pain to stop. Without thinking about the consequences, I searched the medicine cabinet hoping to find sleeping pills. All I found was aspirin and a bottle of Sleep-Eeze. I didn't know what they would do, but I took all the aspirins left, and swallowed as many Sleep-Eeze as I could before a wave of nausea set in. By five o'clock, I was curled up in my bed waiting for my parents to come home, no longer wanting to die and secretly hoping that they would know how to help me.

Around six I heard the car pull into the driveway, the front door close, and my father's voice as he greeted my grandmother. I listened to Dad's heavy footsteps as he headed down the hallway toward my bedroom. The movements were quick. I assumed that my grandmother had told him that I had been in bed since coming home a couple of hours earlier.

My father knocked and then pushed my bedroom door open. "What's the matter? Your grandmother said that you were sick?"

"I swallowed a lot of aspirin and some other pills." I spoke wearily not sure of what else to say.

"You what? How many? Do you feel sick?" The words were tumbling out of Dad's mouth as he moved quickly across the room.

"I'm okay, Dad. I just feel nauseous."

"Sharon, what is wrong with you? Does it have something to do with Michael?" He sat down on the bed next to me. I looked at his tired, worried expression and suddenly regretted what I had done. I felt tears building but nothing happened.

"Why?" he pleaded, suddenly hit with the implications of my actions.

"Michael broke off our engagement," I finally sobbed out.

He must have sensed that there was more. "Why did he do that?"

"Oh, Daddy, my life is a mess. Michael has never forgiven me for having sex with Lenny."

"I suppose he told you that he had never had sex before, right?"

"Yes," I sobbed, thankful that he had not lectured me on the perils of premarital sex. I was already consumed with guilt, feeling that I had made an unwise decision that colored the remainder of my life. Now, the fear of disclosure had me locked in a private hell. With my father near, I wept quietly.

"That's a lie. Sharon, you don't need Michael. He was lucky to have you. You're a special, wonderful girl. Someday, you'll fall in love again and be loved in return." Dad spoke reassuringly.

I was sincerely moved by my father's support. He said all the right things, without judgment, and I had to admit feeling better. Dad bent to kiss me.

"Do you feel well enough to come to dinner?" Dad asked with a warm smile.

"Not really. I mean . . . I'm okay but I would rather stay in bed. Do you mind?"

"No, stay where you are. Want me to have Grandma send you in a plate?" Dad's eyes smiled lovingly.

"Thanks. But, no, I'm not hungry."

A part of me wanted to tell my father about the time Michael had purposely shut my fingers in the car window, cranking it tight while I screamed out in pain. Or the time he twisted my arm behind my back and held it so tight that I cried for mercy. But the incidents didn't seem to matter at that point. I was more relieved to hear my father say that I was still worth something. Besides, I didn't have a clue as to the real reasons for Michael's abusive behavior and couldn't begin to explain it to anyone else, especially my dad.

My father helped me live through that critical moment. However, my self-esteem had a long way to go before I would have the strength required to leave Michael. Typically, Michael and I got back together again and entered one of our periods of calm. While we never did find the ring, our love and affection for each other were rekindled. I decided to cherish the moment and stop fearing the future.

As my graduation from high school drew near, my parents gave me permission to spend a month in Los Angeles with my mother's younger brother, Raymond. We all thought some distance and a change of scenery would help ease the tension. Michael made plans to spend the summer near me in Santa Barbara.

My father was scheduled to play in a golf tournament in Spain. Mom and David were going to accompany him there and then go on to Africa. They planned to go on a safari in East Africa and then fly back across the continent to spend a few days with Ambassador Franklin Williams and his family in Ghana. They invited me along, but I chose a trip alone to California instead.

After the ceremony, we all gave a sigh of relief that I had at least graduated from high school. Mom and Dad gave me a diamond heart, which I still have. It was a peace sign, which I accepted knowingly. Shortly after the ceremony we parted on our respective journeys.

Uncle Raymond and his family welcomed me into their home with few questions, accepting me in spite of my aloofness. My uncle had received accounts of my turbulent last two years from my mother, and yet I felt he understood me even without having heard my side of the story.

For a few weeks, I was happy. Michael and I maintained a level of peace. We explored the coastline together, caught up in the beauty and tranquillity that only the ocean can provide. We were free, in a sense, for the first time in our relationship.

But it wasn't long before reality set in. Neither Michael nor I had been able to find jobs. We had each come to California with some savings, but the money was rapidly dwindling. I could feel the tension building but hoped that we could avoid the eruption.

One evening we went to the movies. After the show we drove around discussing our plans. I wanted to get a job in a department store or grocery, anything to bring in some income; I felt guilty about not making a contribution to Uncle Raymond's household. Michael didn't want me to work in a store. We began to argue. Michael took me back to my uncle's house.

We exchanged angry words on the back steps. Michael put an end to the conversation by punching me so hard in the jaw that the impact of the blow knocked me over onto the concrete steps, where I blacked out.

When I came to I was alone, still sprawled on the steps. I stag-

gered into the house, groggy, trying to recall the events of the
evening. The house was dark and quiet. I went into the living room
and looked out the window. First I spotted the car, still parked in
front of the house. Then I saw Michael. He sat on the curb, with a
knife. He was slowly turning the knife in his hands, over and over.

I was afraid that Michael might attempt to harm himself, so I
woke up my uncle. I briefly described Michael's despondent and
destructive state of mind and asked him to talk to Michael. I didn't
tell Uncle Raymond that Michael had left me unconscious on the
back steps.

I watched from the living room as Michael and Uncle
Raymond sat together on the curb, talking for about ten minutes.
Finally, they stood up, shook hands; Michael got into his car, and
drove off. Uncle Raymond came back into the house and said that
Michael was all right, but Uncle Raymond added that he hoped
we would get our lives straight. I thanked him and went to bed.
After staying with my uncle for a few weeks, I visited my father's
second cousin Daisy Condon in Compton. She lived with her
husband. Their only child was grown and away in the service.
Daisy fussed over me. She cooked and lavished me with affection.
I was thankful for her warmth. When Daisy invited me to come
and stay with her for a while, I happily agreed.

I had been at Daisy's only a week when my father called unex-
pectedly. He had returned home ahead of my mother and brother.
"You know, there has been no word from your brother in months.
I'm really worried," Dad confessed.

"Have you been by the pool hall?" I asked, knowing Jackie's
hangouts as well as my dad.

"I was by there yesterday. No one's seen him. Or so they tell me.
I never know if those guys at the pool hall are lying. I wish that
your mother was here. She'd know what to do."

Dad was pleased that I was in Daisy's loving hands. I assured him
that I was fine. Over the next week, Dad and I spoke at least once
a day and often twice. He was missing Mom and feeling lonely and
I was feeling lost, so our phone calls were mutually beneficial.

It was almost August and I had not found a school for the fall.

Before I had left for the West Coast I had promised my parents that I would explore the California junior college system. With their open admissions policy, Michael and I would be able to go to the same college. The problem was that most of them were day schools with no dormitory facilities and Michael and I needed to board. Dad and I talked about our difficulty finding the right school. I told him that I wanted to give it one last try; I was determined to find a way to remain on the West Coast.

On Sunday, I reviewed the want-ads. The extent of my marketable skills was one semester of high school typing and a year as a nurse's aide. I figured I needn't apply for a secretarial position, and the hospitals wanted LPN's. But an ad for X-ray technicians caught my attention. Monday morning I was on the phone calling programs. By noon I had an appointment to visit a school. The program was three months long and then they helped place you with a local hospital. I was excited with the option.

When I returned to Daisy's, I called Dad and told him about the program, embellishing it with the infinite possibilities, though all the while assuring him that this was only a stop-gap measure, a means to an end, a survival mechanism. An hour later, Dad was back on the phone informing me that he would be in Los Angeles the next day.

Dad's arrival was a relief. He stayed at Daisy's house with me and I enjoyed listening to them catch each other up on their lives. Dad and I spent most of our time around the house talking about my plans for the fall, Jackie's continued disappearance, and Mom's return. By the end of his visit, I was enrolled in the X-ray technician program, and Dad had decided to call my mother in Africa and ask her to shorten her trip and come home to help him locate Jackie. Mom came back immediately, and David, who was fourteen at the time, stayed on for an extra two weeks with the Williamses.

By the time Mom came home, I had moved from Daisy's and was staying in a spare bedroom in Michael's aunt's house in Santa Barbara. The aunt made it clear that she was not happy with me staying in her house. I lasted a week before being farmed out to some of her friends in the community. I was uncomfortable in

Santa Barbara because I had no family or friends in the area. My only connection to the community was through Michael's family. Remembering his mother's theory of the Bible's protectiveness, I went into a religious bookstore and purchased a small white travel Bible and carried it with me at all times. At night, I placed it under my pillow and believed myself safe.

My mother did not approve of the X-ray technician program. She insisted that I find a college with a dorm. Meanwhile, Michael had located LaSalle, who was attending a junior college in Yuma, Arizona, on a basketball scholarship. The school had open admissions, dormitories, and a spot on the basketball team. Within two weeks of his call, Michael and I had our acceptance letters and I could call my mother with the news. We met in Los Angeles and flew to Yuma in time for registration. I was off to college in a small town in the middle of the desert, with cactus trees as tall as buildings, and scorpions in the dormitory gardens.

My mother came with me, and stayed long enough to see that I was enrolled and settled. I was truly grateful for her presence and acceptance of this move. She departed reasonably assured that I would survive the desert climate, but held the door open for me to come home at any point.

From the beginning, Michael made it clear that he was not thrilled about my attending college. He told me he didn't want me to have a career. To ease his fears, I took only home economics courses the first semester—cooking, child development, preschool education, and freshman English. Michael took an equally unchallenging curriculum and was on the basketball team.

But my classes were fun, and I was excited about what I was learning. By the end of the day I was espousing some new theory on child development or describing the use of displacement when measuring a solid like shortening. I aced my first exams and eagerly began to prepare my first case study. My exuberance increased Michael's concerns. After one month, he informed me that we were not staying at Arizona Western for the year. He wanted to elope in January as soon as I turned eighteen.

One weekend Michael and I drove our VW Bug down to

Mexico and got married. Well, we thought that we had gotten married. As it turned out, the justice of the peace was drunk and put the wrong names on our marriage certificate. We should have suspected something would go wrong. The man had stood before us, pronouncing us man and wife with his shirttail hanging out of his pants. When I returned to the dorm, I told my roommate about the ceremony and showed her our marriage license. We cracked up when we read the names on the certificate. Even Michael thought it fitting, given the absurdity of the day. Since the license was a farce there was no need to tell our parents about the failed elopement.

As the semester progressed and I continued to get good grades, Michael became more insecure. One day he announced that he wanted me to leave school early and go to Los Angeles to find a job. The plan was that I would work and he would go to school. He thought that it would be easier for me to find a job than him. Michael told me that he would join me in January after the semester was over. I pleaded with him to be allowed to complete the semester.

Michael gave in, but he also tightened the screws: Friendships, male or female, were not allowed. Nor was any participation in campus life. No parties, no socializing with others in the cafeteria, no membership in clubs. He watched every move I made. Michael vacillated between being loving and cruel. A protective man who could tell me that he loved me and a man who would threaten me with a knife. I never knew which Michael would come out.

One of the basketball players, a sophomore from New York, came to me one day to express his concern about the way Michael kept me under control. He mentioned that I seemed meek and submissive in his presence and he asked me if I was afraid of Michael. I downplayed his concerns and thanked him for his consideration. We spoke a few times after that, but I was always looking over my shoulder. I was lonely and desperate for friendship, yet terrified of the rage it might provoke in Michael.

One day Michael saw me talking with a small group of people in front of my dorm. He grabbed me and slapped me in front of the others. I ran to my room, humiliated. I'd stepped out of line and talked with a boy, so after that incident Michael decided that he needed to assert his authority further. He purchased a rusty old machete which he kept in the car next to the driver's seat. The knife mostly served as a reminder to me to watch my step, but if he felt the urge, Michael would click it up one more notch; he would take me out to the middle of the desert and threaten to stab me with it.

Midway through the semester, my parents called to say that they had to be in Phoenix for a weekend and invited me to join them. I flew to Phoenix feeling better than I had in a long time, relieved to be away from Michael. I ran into my parents' arms, elated to be in their secure boundaries. Our time together was easy for the first time in years. We talked without either side feeling defensive. I came close to telling my mother and father the truth about my relationship with Michael.

They must have sensed my urgency, since we talked of my coming home, and I considered returning to Connecticut with them and not going back to school. I came close, but I didn't tell them. I only alluded to problems between Michael and me. But after a two-hour discussion, we decided finishing the semester was the most responsible thing to do.

I returned to Arizona Western and immediately fell back under Michael's control. He made his ritual promise to be better, I made my ritual acceptance of his words. But time was growing tight, as Michael planned to elope for real this time as soon as I turned eighteen.

A few weeks later, with Michael standing over my shoulder, I called my parents and told them of our plans to elope. They were disappointed and puzzled by my change of heart, but they made one last request. They asked me to return to the East Coast. They promised us a spring wedding.

10

The Arrest

There are three answers which men can make to violence:
revenge, flight, turning the other cheek.

Giovanni Papini, *The Life of Christ*

Mom and Dad had made my April 27 wedding plans contingent
upon my getting a job, and now I had seven weeks to go. I had
worked hard to get my parents up to this level of acceptance,
despite my own nagging doubts about Michael. I was still in love
and determined to go through with the marriage.

I pulled into the parking lot of Norwalk Hospital twenty minutes early. I decided to wait, happy to have a moment to myself
before I had to face the personnel director. I was finding out that
I didn't have many job options.

I still remember the song that was playing on the radio.
"Nothing you can do can take me away from my guy . . . my guy."
I sang along, tapping my foot, when the music stopped abruptly
and a male voice cut in:

"We interrupt this program for a special report. Stay tuned for
details."

I reached out to change channels, but my hand stopped in mid-

air. "A report has just come over the wires stating that Jackie
Robinson Jr. has been arrested. Jackie Robinson Jr., twenty-one-
year-old son of baseball great Jackie Robinson, is being held at the
Stamford jail, charged with two counts of possession of narcotics
and carrying an Italian-made twenty-two-caliber revolver."

I froze. Powerless, I sat there listening, thinking how worried
Mom and Dad had been lately. We hadn't seen Jackie in weeks.

"According to police, young Robinson was apprehended early the
morning of March 4, after police chased him from outside the
Allison-Scott Hotel to nearby South Street. After being frisked,
Robinson was found to have several bags containing heroin, and a
tobaccolike container, possibly marijuana. The young Robinson is
being held in the Stamford jail pending a five-thousand-dollar bond."

I felt hot. Sick. I wanted to scream at someone. Cry out. Blame
the faceless-nameless voice on the radio. Smash the dashboard.
Crawl into a hole. Angry but unsure at whom, frightened and suddenly nauseous, I reached for the ignition, put the car in reverse,
and drove out of the parking lot.

Calm down. Forget the job interview. Mom and Dad need you.
Jackie needs you. My God, Jackie's probably in a jail cell.

The tears fell. I reached for the napkin left over from my lunch
and blew my nose. I dreaded seeing the pain in my parents' eyes.
How many times had I seen it before, over something far less significant? Jackie had been in and out of trouble for as long as I
could remember.

I wondered if my parents had heard the news of Jackie's arrest
from a DJ, as I had. David was miles away, a freshman at Mount
Hermon prep school in Massachusetts. I was glad he wouldn't have
to see his brother behind bars.

I considered stopping at a gas station to call my dad at his office,
but I decided to follow my first instinct and headed straight home.

Driving in a near-daze, I maneuvered my way through the
streets of Norwalk blinded by tears. A troubling conversation I'd
had with Michael the week before returned hauntingly:

"The word on the street is that your brother is using drugs,"
Michael said with concern.

"Rumors," I said, feeling defensive. "Who told you?"

"Heard it when I was playing ball," Michael replied.

I had to pass right by Michael's neighborhood. Part of me wanted to go to him. But I couldn't take the chance of missing Mom and Dad.

I remembered all the times my parents would send me out looking for my brother, hoping that I'd luck into more information through friends that Jackie and I had in common. They were wild-goose chases. But sometimes, after leaving word at various spots on my treks around town, Jackie would call home. He'd say he was all right, and then we wouldn't hear from him again for a couple of weeks. The tension at home was unbearable.

And now it had finally exploded, and worse yet, was all over the news. I pulled into the circular stone driveway that led to our house. My eyes scanned the property searching for answers: Evergreen trees and seemingly endless woods provided privacy and seclusion. Six acres of manicured lawns created the impression of grandeur and expansion. The white pines we had planted as children were now over ten feet tall.

We had so much. Yet it obviously wasn't enough.

As I turned the bend and came from behind the trees I spotted Mom and Dad. They stood on our front steps talking. My knees felt shaky as I climbed out of the car. We hugged. "How did you hear?" Dad asked.

"On the radio. What about you?"

"A reporter called me at the office. Wanted to get my reaction," Dad said, shaking his head. Dad was then special assistant for community affairs to New York governor Nelson Rockefeller. "I called your mother hoping to get to her before she heard it from a stranger."

"Your father and I are on our way to get Jackie out of jail and take him to Yale New Haven Hospital," Mom said, her voice as shaky as my knees. "I've made arrangements for him to be admitted. Do you want to come?"

Jackie was going to be transferred from a jail to a hospital. I wanted to ask about his health, but thought better of it. I couldn't

even form the questions. So I sat in the backseat of Dad's car feeling confused and nervous, terrified of what we would find. How
did someone on drugs look? He must be really sick if Mom and
Dad were taking him right to the hospital. I'd never been inside a
jail. My mind wouldn't stop. My hands were sweating, my stomach
hurt, my eyes burned. No one spoke on the way downtown. By
the time Dad pulled up to the curb in the front of the red-brick
jailhouse my emotions were out of control.

Dad took our arms and we began the slow walk toward the
entrance. What seemed like thousands of reporters, TV cameramen, and photographers pressed in with noise, confusion, insensi-
tivity, and even glory in our pain. I had none of my father's
experience with the press. I saw them then as the enemy, propelled
by blind ambition, supported by their belief in the public's right to
information. What about our right to privacy I wanted to shout.
What about compassion? Human kindness? A few moments to
take in all that we had learned? Time to get my sick brother to the
hospital?

I hated the press. Rage became my overriding emotion. My face
felt hot, lips tight, hands cold. I wanted to cry, scream, run, hide,
hit. I wanted to lash out at someone to ease the pain I was feeling.
My father felt the tension mount; he held tight to my arm as the
reporters persisted in firing questions, snapping pictures and
obstructing our path.

"Mr. Robinson, where were you when you heard the news?"
one reporter asked with a microphone extended toward my
father's lips so he had to say something.

"Did your son call you?" another reporter asked, jamming his
microphone in next to the other.

"Not now, fellas. My wife, daughter, and I just need to see our
boy," Dad responded, just choking his words out as he steadily
guided Mom and me toward the jail. He didn't pause, but Dad's
five-eleven frame was stooped from the repeated surgery on his
right knee that had left him with a permanent limp. The ten feet
of sidewalk seemed like a mile.

One particularly irritating reporter put his face right into ours, determined to get his questions answered. Mom's stoic expression didn't change. Dad maintained his well-trained poise.

I couldn't take any more. I swung my right leg in an effort to kick the man in his shin. Dad pulled me back before I connected.

"Don't let him get to you," Dad whispered.

Don't let him get to you. It was the same control he had shown so many times during his baseball career. The same control that was, I would later think, both his power and his burden. The control that would help improve the lives of countless numbers of people—black, white, or otherwise—but that would at times make it difficult for him to embrace his own son.

I would later realize that for us, the Robinson family, this day was a watershed. After this day, our lives would change forever. After this day, things wouldn't always be better, but they would be more honest, more open. Less . . . controlled.

But at the time, I simply couldn't believe what was happening— my beloved brother was in jail! Behind bars, somewhere in this cold, mean-looking building, locked up. It was a nightmare. I don't remember what Dad said to the officer, I was too nervous, too scared. When a police officer finally escorted us to Jackie in his concrete cell below ground, I gasped and began to sob. Mom was crying, too. We couldn't even hug him. Dad fought to keep his emotions in check. Mom, with tears streaming down her face, reached through the iron bars and grasped Jackie's hand. It was a minute before anyone could even speak.

"Are you all right, son?" Dad asked, clearing his throat.

I searched Jackie's eyes. They were red, watery, as though he'd been crying or had a bad cold. Through sniffles, he nodded yes.

In his defense he told how the policemen shot at him. I flinched, realizing how close we'd come to losing him.

I cried out, "They had no right!"

What we didn't know was that Jackie was firing back at the police, while trying to flee from the scene of a drug bust. It would be years before I heard the whole story of that day—and others.

Mom and I stayed with Jackie while Dad went back upstairs with the officer to place the bond. He was gone for nearly a half hour. He had to fight his way through the army of press again, so he agreed to an impromptu news conference in a police head-quarters room, hoping we would then be left alone to get Jackie to the hospital.

"My wife and I were probably away too much, instead of being home where we were needed," he said. "We obviously have failed someplace. I guess I thought my family was secure and had nothing to worry about. I went running around everywhere else," he continued, shaking his head. "We'll stick with him all the way, regardless of the outcome."

The reporters were satisfied. They had gotten their story. They stepped back as Jackie was released and we went on our way to New Haven. I sat in the back with Jackie, acutely aware of every twitch in his body. There was dead silence in the car during the forty-five-minute drive.

Jackie was admitted to a secured psychiatric ward at Yale New Haven Hospital. I listened as the psychiatrists explained what medication would be used to ease Jackie's heroin withdrawal. They estimated that Jackie would be hospitalized for four to six weeks, receiving therapy daily. We kissed Jackie good-bye, hopeful that he could be helped.

It felt strange leaving Jackie at Yale; Mom was on the faculty and was the Director of Nursing for the Connecticut Mental Health Center. She would have to return the next morning and face her colleagues, knowing that her eldest child was in the hospital across the street, slowly withdrawing from a drug that had nearly consumed his life. Mom, who was usually concerned about appearances, was also incredibly strong and able to keep her family concerns separate from work. Her colleagues were also extremely supportive, attentive, and instructive, helping her to understand that drug addiction is a disease.

To me, it was a relief to know, for the first time in two years, where Jackie was spending the next six weeks and that he was safe.

It was dark by the time my parents and I were back on the Merritt Parkway headed home. My body ached. I closed my eyes, thankful for the end of the day. I couldn't sleep. Something was still gnawing at me. The day had been a complete shock to my system. I felt like a different person. As though, in the space of eight hours, I had grown up. And while thankful that Jackie would be given a second chance, I also realized that though he was out of jail, he was not free of the pain that had allowed drugs to overtake him in the first place. The drugs that had taken over his life.

That was it. I thought about my life with Michael. The amount of control I had conceded to him. I was no more in control of my life than Jackie was of his. And I began to cry quietly, admitting to my own pain if only to myself. Jackie was going to have to accept the responsibility for his own life. So would I.

The doctors had said that they would try to help Jackie find the cause of his drug use, but that he had to want to stop. It seemed like an odd thing to say. My initial reaction was, "Of course he wants to stop. What fool would risk going back to jail?"

Now I thought of my situation: How many times had I tried to leave Michael? How many times had I gone back to a man who terrorized me with threats of physical harm?

When I saw my brother behind bars, something inside me snapped. I wasn't sure where the events of the day would lead. I didn't know if this was the beginning or the end. I couldn't speak for my brother.

But of one thing I was certain: Michael had abused me for the last time.

11

Nineteen Hundred and Sixty-Eight

In spite of my proclamation, I still went shopping for my wedding dress because my love for Michael though no longer blind was strong. Even with my nagging doubts, I still wanted to marry him. My mother remarked in a final effort to get me to change my mind that our visit to the bridal shop was one of the saddest days of her life. Actually, Mom's voice echoed my own inner voice. I just couldn't admit it.

A week later, the six o'clock news was full of accounts of the assassination of Dr. Martin Luther King Jr. For the next twenty-four hours, I sat mesmerized in front of the television, watching the country erupt into violence. Chicago, Baltimore, Washington, D.C., and Cincinnati—the list of cities under siege grew by the minute. Windows were smashed. Stores looted. People were beaten, jailed, and killed. Two black students from Mississippi Valley State College were shot. Students at Florida A & M fired guns and bows and arrows at the police. Fifty people were injured in

Washington, D.C., and ninety were arrested in the Bedford-Stuyvesant section of Brooklyn.

I cursed silently. Caught up in a personal hell, I had been removed from the civil rights movement that had spread across college campuses and the streets of most of the cities. Here I was, the daughter of a great man, practically glued to a black leather couch in our house's library while others were out putting their lives on the line for freedom. My attention to the news was interrupted only by the ringing of the phones. My mother and father watched the accounts from their bedroom.

Meanwhile, I vacillated between a desire to cancel the wedding and my obsession with going forth with the marriage. I still had serious doubts about Michael's ability to keep his promise to me that the violence would cease with marriage, but he had actually been wonderful since our return. There were no arguments. We made joint plans. He seemed less possessive and more open to my family.

Tired of wrestling with myself, I dialed Candy's number. She was home on spring break from her freshman year at Radcliffe.

"Candy, what are you up to?"

"Not much. I thought I would go downtown and see a movie. Are you getting excited about the wedding?"

"More nervous than excited," I admitted.

"Everyone gets nervous before their wedding and yours is only a couple of weeks away." Candy spoke with compassion, thinking that I just needed some encouragement.

"I suppose, but if I'm this nervous do you think that I should go through with the marriage?" I knew that Candy didn't have all the facts in order to make a good judgment, yet I didn't offer her any more details.

"It's pretty late to cancel. You've talked nonstop about this marriage for a year. You're probably feeling the pressure from your parents," she offered, hoping to quell my fears.

Candy was right in one respect. My wedding was practically there. The gown was ordered. Honeymoon paid for. Bridesmaids' dresses being altered. Guests invited. Presents already arriving.

Governor Nelson Rockefeller was coming. Even my parents had come around somewhat. They had decided to give us a honeymoon trip to the Bahamas for a wedding present.

So, on April 27, 1968, I wore a beautiful wedding gown, covered my face with a veil, and marched down the aisle on my father's arm before a packed North Stamford Congregational Church. Dad smiled reassuringly, but I sensed his reluctance as he handed me over to Michael.

Returning from a week in Nassau, I settled into the role of Mrs. Michael Williams with resignation. I got busy creating a comfortable home for us in the miniature attic apartment we shared in Michael's brother's house.

I had finally gotten a job at the phone company six weeks before the wedding but I quit after we married and instead took on the responsibility of caring for two of Michael's nephews. Knowing how opposed Michael was to my working outside of the home, I baby-sat in our apartment thinking that my presence would make Michael happy.

My first visitors were my father and David. They came to dinner one evening when neither Michael nor my mother were available. A relatively inexperienced cook, I prepared a chicken casserole with cream of chicken soup mixed with egg noodles. Dad and I found it amusing that David, not trusting my experiment, opted to stand by the stove and eat the chicken that I had not peeled from the bones. We had a good laugh. But the really funny part of the meal was my apple pie. I had mistakenly used cake flour for the crust. It was a disaster. My father was a good sport though and he good-naturedly ate everything I offered him pretending that it was good.

I saw baby-sitting as a temporary solution. I wanted to return to college. I had learned my lesson about the prospects of finding work without a college degree. So I applied to the University of Bridgeport's associate degree nursing program for the fall. Meanwhile Michael planned to join the Marines. This macho image fit with his ideal of manhood and his eyes would glisten as he described the Marine uniform. The fact that America was in the midst of protests over the Vietnam War didn't faze him. He was ready to serve. Despite the danger and all else I knew about the war, I felt hopeful at his news. It was the first time since his basketball days that I felt him passionate about something. I supported his plan, thinking that it would also free me to go on to college.

The marriage was good for the first couple of months. We shared playful and loving moments and talked openly about our life together. But Michael did not like his job, and soon I began to sense the tension building. I braced myself for the inevitable explosion.

It came one morning while I was in the kitchen preparing breakfast. Michael burst into the room breathing heavily and looking angry. I purposely kept my back to him as the words tumbled out. Mean words. Words meant to enrage. Words designed to sting. But this time I didn't fold into a fetal position. I stood straight. I had no idea what brought this attack on—it certainly wasn't the fact that he didn't want fried eggs and bacon as he claimed.

While Michael ranted, I kept stirring the eggs and turning the popping bacon. My pulse raced. All the while I was thinking, He doesn't realize that I am a changed person. This is a test and I am going to let him know that it won't work anymore . . . I turned around, graceful and deliberate. My hands were perched defiantly on my hips. I finally shouted back, "You will not treat me like a dog anymore, I am your wife now . . ." This was the first time I had confronted Michael. In the past, he had used exposing the fact that I was not a virgin to threaten me. Marriage had removed the basis of that threat. Virginity was no longer an issue. I was a married woman. Finally, believing in my right to respect, I felt strong and willful again. Neither his words nor his size intimidated me. Amazing, I thought, grinning inside . . . I can do this.

I had no idea how Michael would respond to the new me. Marriage had done nothing for his security or self-esteem. He still needed to be in control of me through verbal and physical measures. In a matter of months, I had grown up and stopped being afraid. Self-control was my goal.

Michael left for work without finishing breakfast. However, the moment he entered the house that evening I knew that the battle was not forgotten. I was ready. I shielded my face with a pillow as he knocked me onto the bed. Using my defense against me, he pushed the pillow against my face, making it difficult to breath. He was much stronger, but I had years of anger on my side. Finally, landing a good kick to his abdomen, Michael backed off, freeing me to run.

I tore down the narrow staircase that led to the main part of the house. Michael was hot on my heels. We simultaneously burst into his brother's kitchen where the family had gathered for dinner.

"George, please take me home!" I shouted, almost incoherent with rage.

"You're not going anywhere!" Michael shouted back.

"What's going on?" George asked, standing and moving toward us.

"This marriage is over!" I screamed.

George pulled Michael out of the kitchen and into the living room. I stayed in the kitchen and allowed George's wife to console me.

In the middle of our discussion, George walked back into the kitchen with his arm wrapped around his subdued brother. Michael apologized. George then tried to explain away Michael's behavior as job-related. I retorted, "Taking care of two toddlers in a tiny apartment is not my idea of glory either, but it's a job."

George again assumed the voice of reason. He told me that he had offered Michael a job with his trucking company. He explained that Michael would start as a truck driver but assured us both that if it worked out he could grow with the company. Michael seemed pleased with the idea. Michael wasn't ready to join the Marines, so he accepted George's offer.

The tension between Michael and me was broken. We talked for half an hour with George and his wife, finally agreeing to go back upstairs and to give our marriage time.

For the next month, life proceeded in relative tranquillity until I got word that my dad had suffered a mild heart attack. The doctors said it was a warning. Dad was ordered to take it easy and remain at home for a few weeks. During his recuperation I tried to keep the news light and pleasant. It worked until all hell broke loose in my marriage for the second time. Michael arrived home swinging at me in an uncontrollable rage.

I sought refuge behind a chair, angling it protectively in front of my body. My back was to the wall. Michael kicked with a mounting fury that grew from an inability to reach his target. The furious attack must have lasted five minutes. Finally, his rapid deep breathing was the only sound in the room. I peered from behind the chair and gasped. Blood was streaming down my husband's leg yet he hadn't even noticed the gash on the inner surface of his ankle. I pointed toward the wound.

"Michael, look what you've done to yourself! When the fury comes over you everything else is blocked out. You need to get some help." I spoke softly, emerging from behind the chair and heading to the bathroom for a towel to wrap his leg.

"You're right to leave me." Michael sounded resigned. He stood shaking his head. There was no need for more words.

"Do you want me to drive you to the hospital?" I asked, genuinely concerned about his physical condition and depressed state of mind. Michael shook his head. I watched from the upstairs window as he limped to the car and drove away. After the car disappeared, I packed my bags and loaded my car. Unable to see myself fleeing to my parents, I collapsed on the bed trying to come up with an excuse that would satisfy them. I did not want them to know about the beatings. My father had been home on bed rest for the past month recuperating from a mild heart attack and I worried that knowledge of the abuse would set his recovery back. I decided that a morning arrival would attract the least amount of attention and planned to leave then.

Sometime later that night Michael came back to the apartment. His leg was bandaged. The cut had required stitches. We both fell asleep without a word. The next morning, Michael woke up with a kind of amnesia and had no memory of telling me that it was okay for me to leave. I remained calm but firm, telling him that I needed to get some distance so that I could think. I purposely left my plans ambiguous, though I knew as I piled the rest of my things into the car that I would not return. I wanted Michael out of my life forever.

As I merged with the morning traffic on the southbound lane of the Merritt Parkway, my mind was blank. Twenty minutes later, I pulled into my driveway. I was safe. I glanced at my watch. It was nine o'clock. I knew that my mother would already have left for work. My father would be home alone.

I used my key to enter the house.

"Dad, it's me," I called out to my father as I made my way down the hallway toward his room.

"What are you doing home at this hour?" Dad asked as we reached to hug each other.

"Dad, I've left Michael."

"Left? What does that mean? You just got married."

"Dad—it's too hard to explain. I need to just lie down now. Can we talk later?"

"Okay, we'll talk when your mother gets home." Dad accepted what I said on face value. He knew that when my mother arrived I would have to come clean. I couldn't take that risk though, so I planned to be gone by the time she arrived.

Before I took a nap I called Uncle Chuck and Aunt Brenda in Long Island and made arrangements to stay with them. By five o'clock that evening I was sitting at their kitchen table giving my aunt and uncle a capsulized version of my relationship with Michael. They asked questions that I couldn't answer. Why didn't I leave Michael the first time he hit me? Why did I marry him? I shook my head, not knowing the answers. For the time being, I chose to live with my mistake. The whys would have to be answered later. My aunt and uncle assured me that I was welcome to stay with them. For the next two days there were no more questions and no demands placed upon me. I rested and prepared to go back out into the world.

Within a week of my arrival, Uncle Chuck arranged with a local nonprofit organization for me to work for them part-time and took me to register at a local college for summer school. I was thankful for his clear direction, structure, and assistance. I also knew that the next steps were up to me.

The first time I heard Michael's voice on the phone, I trembled. He threatened to come to Long Island to bring me back to Norwalk. I told him that I had no intention of coming back. I hung up the phone in the midst of his threats. Michael called right back. My uncle told me that he would handle Michael. I heard my uncle return my husband's threats with equal strength. He told Michael that he would shoot him if he came near his niece.

Michael must have gotten the message because he didn't call back. The next day, my mother called. Michael had gone to my parents, appealing for their support. He told them that he wanted me back. My mother was calling to ask me to come home so that we could sit down and talk. I knew that it was time to face my parents. I agreed, with the stipulation that Michael not be informed of our meeting.

As I walked into my house the following weekend, I felt the coldness. The barrier between my mother and me had grown thicker, taller. I knew immediately that we would not scale it today. We sat down. I read the disappointment on her face.

Mom did most of the talking. I listened. She said that she and my father didn't understand how I could walk out on a marriage after three months, especially one that I had fought so hard to make happen. Hadn't they asked me not to get married so young? Pleaded with me? Been manipulated by me finally into accepting the marriage, even going so far as to give me a honeymoon? I had no defense. She was right.

Michael had been to see my parents and had described an incident where I kicked him. "Your father and I can't believe that our daughter could do such a thing," Mom said. I stared blankly at my mother, feeling the anger build. "Did you kick Michael?"

"I did. But only because he had a pillow over my face and I would have smothered if I didn't get free." Now, I was really angry. No longer willing to listen. As far as I was concerned, the session was over. I had nothing to say and didn't care to hear what they had to say. I wasn't about to defend myself. Nor reveal the depths of my pain. It is hard to say who I was protecting and who I was punishing: my father, my mother, or myself. I believed that ultimately the abuse reflected negatively on me. Even though I had finally summoned the courage to walk out, I still felt that I must have done something to warrant the attacks.

As I sat across from my mother, I fought with mixed emotions and turned most of my anger on her. I felt like a china doll on the top shelf of a little girl's bookcase whose legs are a little too close to the edge. But it was not this frail image I portrayed that afternoon; it was the stubborn, rigid, defiant side of me that came through.

There were lots of questions for which I had no answers. I felt guilty that my problems were placing an additional burden on an already stressed family and I had a real fear about how the truth would affect my father's health. We discussed my plans to return home at the end of the summer so that I could attend the nursing program at the University of Bridgeport. In the end, I informed them that I would be meeting with a lawyer and hoped to have my marriage annulled. I left them no doubt that it was over.

In August, I had my first appointment with our family lawyer, Sidney Kweskin. I told him everything. He listened without reproach.

After I had told my story, Mr. Kweskin explained matrimonial law. I did not have grounds for an annulment but could file for a divorce on the grounds of physical and mental cruelty. It was the first time I would have a name for Michael's mistreatment. I felt a flood of relief, like the patient with a set of vague symptoms who finally finds a doctor with a diagnosis and a treatment plan.

Kweskin explained the process. I would have to go to court with witnesses who could testify to incidents of abuse. The judge would hand down the ruling. Finally, Mr. Kweskin turned to me and asked me "Why?" for the second time that morning. Only this time it was not why I wanted to end my marriage. He wanted to know why had I married in the first place. I told him that Michael had promised that the abuse would stop after we got married.

Mr. Kweskin made an observation that I have never forgotten.

He said, "During the courtship men are usually on their best behavior." He went on to say that I deserved better. I looked at him in silence, wanting to believe his words. I heard him but could not bring it into my soul. I was still a long way from feeling good about myself.

That fall, I was back in my old bedroom on Cascade Road commuting to the University of Bridgeport and working part-time on the switchboard at the YMCA. Each afternoon I checked the mailbox, hoping to receive word from my lawyer about a court date for my divorce. I wanted that chapter in my life closed for good.

My high school friend Linda and I quickly discovered that we were the only members of our circle of friends who had not gone away to college, and on weekends we often headed to New York City to party. One Friday, Linda and I got into Linda's car and headed to the Columbia University campus, checking out all the now familiar hangouts. Our comrades were nowhere to be found. Linda and I drove aimlessly around the city completely bored. After an hour or so, Linda pulled her father's station wagon up in front of a liquor store on Broadway. I waited in the car. Linda returned with two bottles of Ripple.

Linda knew that I didn't drink alcohol. She thrust one of the bottles toward me telling me to try it. I'd seen Linda and her cousin Ralph indulge in the frothy pink liquid from green-colored bottles many times before. They would be so giggly after a bottle or two. I was tempted by its promise of cheer. I took the bottle, twisted off its cap, and took a big gulp. The cool liquid, which until that moment had been a stranger to me, had an unfamiliar but not necessarily unpleasant taste. With a shrug of my shoulders, I proceeded to drink the entire contents of the bottle much as I would a raspberry soda on a hot summer day. Soon after, I passed out, and the sudden jerking of the car sent my semiconscious body crashing to the floor of the car. Cursing, Linda shouted to me:

"Sharon, get up and hide that bottle! The cops have stopped us." Linda, whose head was considerably clearer than mine, was fumbling through the glove compartment looking for the car registration.

"What did you do?" I asked, shocked back into the present.

"Ran a red light," Linda replied, now sounding nervous. About that time the cops flashed a light into the window on the driver's side. I kept quiet.

Linda adeptly handled the policeman, copping an out-of-town plea. "Sorry, Officer, I'm not familiar with the rapid change in the traffic lights. In Stamford, the small town that we have just come from, traffic lights, when there are any, go from green to yellow to red." I focused straight ahead trying hard to contain my laughter. I was really impressed with Linda's performance. After checking Linda's credentials and giving her a stern lecture, the policeman waved us on.

Linda and I were rebellious and anxious to belong. The activism and revolutionary philosophy of the Black Panthers appealed to our sense of disenfranchisement. We'd begun to feel as if students were active on every campus across the country except ours. We thought about joining one of the civil rights groups and the only organization that appealed to us was the Black Panthers.

To be perfectly honest, I am not sure if it was the black tams, handsome men, or revolutionary rhetoric that we found most attractive, but we went as far as to look into the nearest affiliate. Naturally, there was no chapter in Stamford, Connecticut. Now, if we were truly serious, we could have joined the New York chapter, but that was too intimidating. So instead of joining physically, we joined spiritually. In homage to our leader, Linda and I went into Harlem to our favorite bookstore and purchased an eleven-by-fourteen poster of Huey Newton sitting in that famous rattan chair with his black beret cocked slightly to the side. He was one fine brother! Just as we lay across my bed looking up at our handsome hero, my father knocked on my door. He had just gotten home from work and was stopping off to say hello.

"Come in," I shouted through the closed door. "Oh, hi, Dad." I barely got the greeting out before I noticed my father's eyes rest on our new poster.

"Get that poster off the wall! I will not have that man's face in my house!" Dad shouted. I was shocked. In my lifetime, my father

had denied me only one other thing: a cat. This was the first time
he had ever yelled at me. And to forbid me something simple like
a poster. I was highly incensed, but smart enough to know that I'd
better do as told. The poster came off the wall.

I didn't realize then that my father was also at a critical turning
point in his life. After years of being an activist in the civil rights
movement, he was now finding himself at odds with every organization from the Black Panthers to the NAACP. He felt that the
NAACP had lost touch with the community. Finally, in 1967, my
father had resigned from the NAACP board of directors because
he was frustrated by their growing conservatism and distance from
the black community.

The year before Dr. King's assassination, he and Dad had had a
public disagreement as well. Dr. King's antiwar position had created controversy and debate within the black community. The
NAACP openly opposed King's stance. Even SCLC, Dr. King's
own organization, issued a disclaimer that his position was a personal one and did not necessarily reflect the thinking of the organization. People were confused. Dad dedicated his weekly
newspaper column to the issue by publishing an open letter to
Martin Luther King Jr. He felt that Dr. King's antiwar statement
needed clarification. Before mailing off the letter, Dad tried to
reach Dr. King. His phone calls were not returned. Several days
went by. Feeling as though he had to speak while the issue was
being hotly debated, my father submitted his letter for publication.

"You suggest that we stop the bombing," he wrote. "Why
should we take the vital step of stopping the bombing without
knowing whether the enemy will use that pause to prepare for
greater destruction of our men in Vietnam? Why do you seem to
ignore the blood that is on their hands and speak only of the guilt
of the United States? Why do you not suggest that the Viet Cong
cease, stop, withdraw also? I am confused, Martin," he concluded.
"I am confused because I respect you deeply."

The day after the letter appeared in newspapers across the country, Martin Luther King called my father at home. Dad described
that call, several years later, in his autobiography. "I was terribly

touched by the fact that Martin was not nearly as anxious to defend my attack publicly as he was to have me, as a friend, understand his philosophy and motivation. This was one more attribute of Martin's humanity. Criticism, especially from friends, wounded him deeply."

As it was, the nonviolent visionary refused to back down on his unpopular stance against the war. Dad, the father of a Vietnam veteran, felt equally as strong that the United States should honor its commitment and should not back down in the face of an aggressive enemy. With these very different perspectives on the war, the best these two men could do was to agree to disagree. As private men, friends and fathers, there was too much respect and admiration between them to have it any other way.

By the early seventies, Martin Luther King had proven the wiser. Dad continued in the last few chapters of his book, "I have not embraced nonviolence, but I have become more cynical about this country's role in Vietnam. I have become skeptical about the old domino theory; that the fall of Vietnam would bring communist domination to Southeast Asia. I feel that the regime we are supporting in South Vietnam is corrupt and not representative of the people. I am particularly upset by the plight of the black soldier. I cannot accept the idea of a black supposedly fighting for the principles of freedom and democracy in Vietnam when so little has been accomplished in this country. There was a time when I deeply believed in America. I have become bitterly disillusioned."

Dad was falling out with everybody. He took on Macolm X around the same time. Dad basically felt the militancy of the Black Panthers would never work in the black community, but felt equally certain that the other black organizations of the times were not meeting the needs of the people. He did not embrace ideologies of violence, or black nationalism, or black separatism. In 1963, Malcolm X had insulted Dr. Ralph Bunche, the then undersecretary of the United Nations, by saying he made statements to please white people. My father and Malcolm X had had a shouting match via the newspaper expressing their differences. Outraged by Malcolm X's attack on Dr. Bunche, Dad wrote a column in his defense. Malcolm X responded in writing with a scathing attack on my father. Dad wrote back thanking Malcolm X for putting him in such distinguished company as Dr. Bunche, Roy Wilkins, Dr. King, and Mr. Randolph. So the poster symbolizing all that he opposed was a sore point and one not worth fighting over.

In September, my lawyer filed my divorce papers. Preparing me for the hearing, he said that I would need two witnesses. Michael had been careful. There were no eyewitnesses.

After my meeting with Mr. Kweskin, I went home and sat down with my mother to discuss, in peace, the divorce. She asked me if the bruises she had observed on my arms were associated with Michael. I admitted, without going into detail about specific incidents, that they were. I needed to say no more. Mom volunteered to testify to the presence of bruises. I asked Linda to do the same. All that was left was to wait for the judge to assign me a court date. I had nightmares. One was of the judge telling me I would have to give my marriage another try. Another was that the press had gotten word of my impending hearing and were lined up as we entered the courtroom, ready to pounce.

It took months, but finally I was given a court date. The wait had given me time to begin to heal and I was feeling good. I loved school and I was getting good grades. With Michael out of my life, the source of much of the tension between my parents and me was kept at a minimum. Mom was pleased that I was attending college and Dad seemed happy to have me back at home.

Despite my newfound confidence, on May 1, the morning of the trial, I woke up a mass of nerves. Mom, Linda, and I arrived at Superior Court in Stamford at 9 A.M., not knowing when we would be called. We had all agreed that it was best for my father not to come to the courthouse with us. I didn't want him to hear the testimony and we hoped to keep news of the divorce proceedings from the press. It worked. There was no press and no mention of Jackie Robinson in the courtroom. We took a seat next to our lawyer and friend. I listened to the cases in front of me, growing more anxious with each testimony. I had never been that nervous in my life, and I hated knowing that the judge held my life in his hands. I made three trips to the ladies' room to vomit. Finally, the court recorder called out, "*Williams v. Williams.*"

My mother and Linda testified to seeing the aftereffects of the abuse—the bruises. When I took the witness seat, I couldn't control my shaking. I had never had my behavior and decision-making under such scrutiny. I was petrified; especially when I realized that the judge could turn down my request for a divorce.

I tried to calm my voice and tell my story. Mom and Linda had done the same. The proceedings lasted only a matter of minutes. I looked the judge in the eye as he handed down the ruling. Without hesitation, he granted me a divorce, citing intolerable cruelty. I was permitted to return to the use of my maiden name. I left the courtroom legally divorced at nineteen, but hardly free of the pain, the guilt, the unresolved anger or even, I realized as I continued for months to look over my shoulder, the fears.

February 10, 1946: The marriage of Jackie Robinson and Rachel Isum. *Left to right:* Florence Nukes, Flora Boswell, Buddy Devine, Pete McCullough, Rachel, Sid Heard, Jackie, Jack Gordon, Charlotte Robinson, Josephine Marshall.

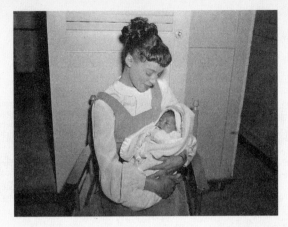

In Hollywood on the set of *The Jackie Robinson Story.* I'm sleeping peacefully in the arms of Ruby Dee.

Dad's publicity shot for *The Jackie Robinson Story* in 1950.

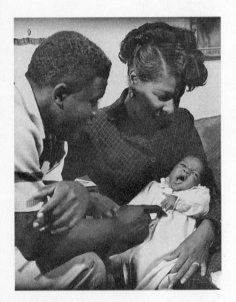

Dad, Mom, and me in a photo taken for *Life* magazine.

The Brooklyn Dodgers vs. the New York Yankees—Snutty Stirnweiss watches as Dad slides into second, and shortstop Phil Rizzuto becomes airborne trying to tag him.

The Brooklyn Dodgers vs. the Cincinnati Reds—from second base, Dad throws to first, forcing out Johnny Temple. (United Press Photo)

Four generations—my grandmother Zellee Islum, me, Mom, my great-grandmother Annetta Jones, and Jackie Jr.—pose for photographer Inge Hardison in our St. Alban's home in 1951.

Jackie Jr. and me horsing around with Dad for the cameras.

Dad and me in the Miami sun at spring training.

On the ice at Grossinger's in 1951—young fans were always eager to jump in front of the cameras with Dad.

Jackie Jr. already trying to fill Dad's big shoes at our St. Alban's house with me and Mom.

My brothers and me at home—David had his goofy grin even then.

Spring training bound—Jackie Jr., Mom, me, David Campanella, and Chuckie Williams pose on the train.

I was always enthralled when Dad read to me—especially when we were being taped for TV.

The Robinson
family at dinner
in the
Grossinger's
dining room.

At the construction site of the new house in Stamford in 1954. (*Look* magazine)

Jackie Robinson

Dear Jackie, Sharon and David,

Mommy has been telling how what good children you have been and I am so glad to hear it. I will be coming home in a few days and for being so nice mommy and I will take you to the circus to see the animals, clowns and all the things that go with a circus. I am really proud of all of you and am always telling people I have the best children in the world. I know you are going to be even better and you are going to work real hard to be a lot of friends like mommy and daddy ha——

I know you are remembering you are to———— of the house while I am away and are show—— the others what is right and wrong. Sharon is my big girl and mommy's helper. It's so nice having a girl so she can be the second mommy to look after the others be a big girl and help with David. I know David is growing and is talking a lot now so I hope he keeps it up.

I will be seeing you soon so be good children always.

Love
Dad

One of Dad's famous letters sent from spring training.

Jackie, Sharon and David Robinson
112 - 40 177 Street
St. Albans, New York

The Robinson family trip to Washington, D.C., for our first glimpse at government. Here we are in front of the White House gate in 1957.

On the way to the Hall of Fame induction in 1962—Grandma Mallie, Uncle Mack, and Grandma Zellee.

Dolan Junior High class of 1964—Candy in her headband sits in the front row, second from left, and I'm in the middle of the row, prim and proper in my white dress.

At Grossinger's in 1964—David, me (yes, that's a hat), and Christy on the slopes.

A Jack & Jill group photo—Candy and I sit on the far left, and Candy's stepmother, Gail Allen, stands behind us next to Mom.

Dad walks me down the aisle for my marriage to Michael in 1968.

Mom and Dad on
vacation, relaxing under
the palm trees.

On Christmas Eve 1969: Joe kisses the bride as the minister, Jackie Jr., and Candy look on.

After the wedding, Jackie Jr. gives me his congratulations.

Marian Logan captures our last Thanksgiving with Dad and Jackie
Jr. at the Stamford house in 1970. *Front row:* David, Rudy Gordon,
Jill Gordon (baby), Brenda Williams, Zellee Isum, Rachel, Jackie Jr.,
and me. *Middle row:* Joe, Jackie Sr., Chuckie Williams, Lori Gordon,
Arthur Logan, and Brad Gordon. *Last row:* Chuck Williams and
Jack Gordon.

February 1972: All smiles, Dad shows off his award from Operation
PUSH—with Jesse Jackson, Rachel, and Tom Todd.

Me and my proud mom at Howard
University's graduation in May 1973.

I was happy that
Grandma Zellee lived
long enough to witness
my graduation. Marian
snapped a picture of the
four of us at my nursing
school ceremony.

Taking a moment out from a busy midwifery internship to relax in the Jamaica sunshine.

A photo that accompanied the *Ebony* feature story on the three of us in 1973, one year after Dad's death.

At home in
Stamford in 1979—
me and my giggling
baby Jesse.

David likes to remind Jesse that
there was a time when he carried
him on his back.

At fourteen Jesse towered over
Willette. I cried all the way through
his eighth grade graduation from the
Windward School.

12

Stripped Naked

After two months at Yale New Haven Hospital, Jackie was released and said to be drug-free. Three months later, he was arrested again. This time I was not taken by surprise. Jackie had been missing for weeks and I assumed that the disappearance had something to do with drugs.

Charged with drug trafficking and possession of a pistol without a permit, Jackie pleaded guilty. The superior court judge sentenced him to state prison for two to three years for the first count and one year on the second count. His sentence was commuted to three years of probation when Jackie agreed to go to Daytop, a residential drug treatment facility in Seymour, Connecticut.

I didn't go when Mom and Dad drove Jackie to Daytop, but I waited anxiously for their return. They were exhausted, but convinced that Jackie was in the right place. They tried to prepare me for the next few months. Mom told me that we would keep in touch with Jackie through the staff and it would be a month or longer before he would be allowed to write and call home. Daytop was run by ex-addicts, so they knew their way around the manipulative behavior of addicts. Jackie, like any new recruit, would have to earn privileges.

The early reports were of struggle. Jackie, according to the counselors, resented and rejected the constant probing into his psyche. But, accustomed to resistance, the counselors pressed on. They forced my brother to confront himself, in the hope that he would eventually take responsibility for his own behavior.

The counselors whittled away at the feelings under the surface and insisted that Jackie not hide behind a mask to escape from the pressures of being Jackie Robinson Jr. or use the Vietnam War as an excuse for his drug dependence. The counselors stripped him naked, and told my brother to start fresh.

Now that Jackie's drug addiction and my abusive marriage were no longer secrets, I silently wished that we could be more open with our emotions. But the silence was too well ingrained. The emotions too deeply buried. I often wondered what my mother and father spoke about in the privacy of their room. Did Mom cry out loud, or were the emotions kept inside even then? And what about my father? How did he release his feelings?

One evening after Jackie had been in Daytop for about a month, the director, Kenny, called to warn us that Jackie was about to rebel in the only way he knew: running. Kenny stressed the importance of us not giving in to this behavior because then we would only be reinforcing that running was okay. He advised my parents that when Jackie called saying he planned to leave Daytop, they were to tell him that he could not come home. Mom and Dad were terrified. They felt as though Kenny was telling them to turn their back on their child. What would be the consequence of taking such an extreme position? Where would Jackie go? If he came home, there was a chance that we could talk him into returning. If he went back to the streets, the police would arrest him. He could be jailed or, God forbid, killed while he tried to escape. Each time the phone rang, we jumped, fearing the moment when Jackie would call. I prayed that my parents would answer the phone. I didn't think I had the resolve.

Finally the call came. Mom and Dad listened on separate lines and when he finished, together they told him that he could not come home. The Daytop staff did not try to talk Jackie out of leaving, but they did remind him that breaking his commitment meant that only a jail cell or death would welcome him.

Jackie left Daytop anyway, saying that he had money to collect and people to see and then he would come back. As it turned out, the program was getting through to him, because Jackie stayed away only long enough to tie up the loose ends he had left in the street. Two days later, he arrived back at Daytop's big house on the hill in a white Cadillac. He waved good-bye to the friend who had driven him back to Daytop, and began to settle down with renewed purpose.

Exactly what turned my brother around is a mystery to me. Possibly a combination of tough love and his own will to live. Whatever the turning point, Jackie stopped fighting the rigorous program that forced him to examine himself. He completely withdrew from drugs without methadone, Valium, or alcohol, and he was drug-free for the first time in years.

At home, the house was suddenly lighter, more relaxed, hopeful. We had started to visit Jackie as a family, and listen to him explain his growth. We observed a changed person. We would leave Daytop on a high bolstered by waves of possibility.

Despite all we had to be thankful for, I worried about the toll my brother's and my troubles took on my parents. My father was raised in a Christian home and believed in the power of prayer, but in his adult years his attendance at church had been an occasional activity rather than a regular source of comfort. One of his favorite sayings though was that God was testing him and would not give him more than he could bear. I had my doubts. A heart attack before fifty, diabetes, repeated trouble with his knees. I was worried about losing him.

My concerns about my mother were a different matter. She tended to deal with crises by distancing herself and focusing on those things within her control. In a way, I worried more about her emotional status than I did about my father's because he, at least, relaxed regularly on the golf course or at the racetrack. I wasn't sure how my mother relaxed.

One of the few times I got a true glimpse of my father's inner struggle occurred one evening when he invited me to accompany him on a speaking engagement. I was delighted and didn't bother to ask him about his topic—it didn't matter. On the way, Dad asked me about my nursing classes. I remember we laughed at my descriptions of a film we had seen in our fundamentals class that featured a segment on a colostomy club. I just couldn't see forming a group to sit around and discuss what it was like to live with a colostomy. I didn't really want to confront any of my feelings about my own hurts and bitterness, so I couldn't imagine others wanting to share their pain.

The moment we arrived at the auditorium, my father and I were separated. I really didn't mind—over the years I had come to accept that I had to share my father with the world. I watched him handling the attention with smiles and grace. He clearly enjoyed feeling needed.

As the room filled, I took a seat in the middle section several rows from the front. There must have been several hundred people packed into the small school auditorium, most of them white. The mood was serious, almost somber. There was no music. No string of people to precede the main speaker and dilute his presence. The people gathered had come to hear from my father alone. A man I didn't recognize came up to the podium and cleared his throat. The room fell silent.

The moderator represented a parent support group. In his introduction, he spoke of my father's triumphs and tribulations, his peaks and valleys. Eventually, Dad stood and walked slowly to the podium, squinted into the audience, and thanked the people for coming. When Dad introduced me, I stood proudly.

Dad began his speech with his voice choked, his expression serious, and his words chosen to stir. His speech did not have the emotional crescendos of a Baptist preacher, but to me his message was far more striking. He was speaking as a father who had been forced to deal with his son's addiction to drugs. His namesake. The one child he had been alienated from for years. The one he least understood—until now.

Dad tried to keep his voice steady: "I know what it is to wake up one morning and find my whole world, the whole world of those nearest and dearest to me, changed, threatened, transformed, because my son had become addicted."

I twisted nervously. I had never heard him speak about my brother's problems. I wasn't sure if I was going to like hearing what he had to say. I started to resent the faces in the audience. What right did they have to share in our pain?

"My oldest child went to Vietnam when he was seventeen. He was smoking marijuana when he came back. One day marijuana wasn't good enough for him. He turned to heroin, became an addict, ran into all kinds of problems." I wondered if Dad knew that Jackie had smoked marijuana long before going to Vietnam.

"I can remember the first day my son was arrested. I was at my office in New York and I got a telephone call from a newspaperman talking about some of the things that are happening in sports. When he hung up after fifteen or twenty minutes of conversation I was sitting there and the phone rang again. The fellow called back and I thought maybe he forgot to ask me a particular question. His question to me was: 'What about Jackie?' I wanted to know what he was talking about.

"He pointed out that Jackie had been arrested at one the night before—it was eleven-thirty then—and this was the first we'd heard about it. He wanted to know what we were going to do about it."

Dad paused. He cleared his throat and took a drink of water.

"It was such a shock I didn't know what to tell him. My first reaction was, Well, Jackie, you got yourself into very serious trouble, now get yourself out of it. But my wife and I decided that regardless of what the circumstances were, regardless of the problem, that he didn't get into any problems by himself. He got into trouble because of society and because of the very serious problem he has with constantly being compared to me.

"I can't help but feel that had it not been for the fact that both my wife and I decided to stand by Jackie the outcome could have been different. We couldn't be concerned with what the news media was going to say; or how the next-door neighbor would react. We had a youngster who needed help and we had to continue giving him love and understanding. I think this is what the average parent must do. Stick by that youngster no matter how powerful the drug problem might be. It's a serious tragedy and it can be the most devastating thing that can happen to a family, but you can't give up on that youngster."

I wasn't the only one in the room in tears. The man in front of me turned around and looked as though he wanted to say something. He hesitated when he saw the tension in my body and the tears in my eyes. "It must have been hard." He smiled supportively. I nodded. The man turned back around. I was thankful for his smile and kindness. I tensed up more, trying to hold back the tears, thinking tears should only come in private. My father was winding down his talk. His composure amazed me.

"Drug addiction is a tremendous leveler. It is no respecter of color. It is an unfortunate truth. But a truth nonetheless. The sensibilities of our society to the dangers of illegal drug use and abuse were not really aroused so long as drug addiction was presumed to be confined to the poor and the black. But when it was revealed that the monster was attacking in the suburbs as well as the slums; when news articles and television bulletins began to reel off the names of youngsters from rich and famous families as addiction victims; when polls and investigations revealed that addiction was spreading like poison ivy through college campuses and high schools and grammar schools in communities all over the nation, then a mighty concern was generated and we began as a nation to ask ourselves what we had not done, to question ourselves as parents as to how we had failed our children and what we now must do. It seems to me the first look we must take is in the moral mirror."

Dad went on to compare the denial about the prevalence of drug abuse to the failure of Northerners to stand up for the human rights of black people. He accused Northerners of a willingness to write checks to support the civil rights struggle as long as the protest remained in the South. When they found themselves "inconvenienced" or threatened or were asked to give more than token help, it was a different story. Dad's voice was getting stronger. He continued.

"Our country is sick today . . . sick with frustrations, with lack of communication, with war and with all the maladies which our young people confront in their early years. We are drinking our martinis and chain smoking and living off our tranquilizers and sleeping pills and telling so-called white lies and then we are surprised that such disease is contagious; surprised that our young have become defeatist and cynical. They're aware that we tell them to do not as we do but as we tell them to do."

Dad was on a roll. I looked around at the faces, no longer thinking of the audience as a room full of strangers. We had a bond. The tears were now replaced with nodding heads, quiet murmurs of agreement, smiles. Dad didn't want these people to feel sorry for him or even for themselves. He was trying to motivate them into action. There was applause all around me. People jumped up from their seats.

I understood why my father had wanted me to hear him speak: It was easier for him to tell me this way. I was accustomed to Mom and Dad holding in emotions. I was certain that my father believed all that nonsense about men not crying—fathers and sons shaking hands instead of exchanging hugs. That was the way he had lived, in any case.

As Dad descended the short flight of steps that led into the auditorium, a crowd followed him, the people shaking his hand, talking to him. I stayed back, waiting my turn. The desire to run into the safety of his arms urged me forward. Yet I didn't take a step. I waited, confident that my turn would come. I felt flooded with things I wanted to say. When the opportunity presented itself, I couldn't form the words. The pattern of not talking about feelings was so ingrained that I could not release them.

I knew my father felt that he had failed Jackie. In his early years,

Dad was too absorbed in baseball to establish a strong relationship with his firstborn. Later, when Dad had to be the disciplinarian, Jackie wouldn't listen. The estrangement was compounded by the fact it was our father's image from which Jackie was trying to escape. I hoped the doubts and frustrations were behind us now, but as I looked into my father's sad eyes I no longer felt confident that we had survived the hardest part.

13

New Beginnings

Christmas of 1968, Linda's boyfriend, Kenny from Howard, called to say he was bringing home his roommate, Joe, a premed student. Linda, never at a loss for solutions, suggested that we double date.

Joe was thin, close to six feet, with the biggest afro I had seen and a full beard. He reminded me of H. Rap Brown without the glasses. Eleven years my senior, a past disciple of Stokely Carmichael, member of SNCC, and a future doctor, he was too much to ask for. At a glance, he fulfilled both my romantic and revolutionary fantasies.

I was fascinated by and envious of Joe's passionate accounts of meetings, protests, and interrelationships in the movement. With Joe in my life, who needed a Huey Newton poster? I was so caught up in the passion Joe exuded in describing the past, that I didn't think how it might apply to the present, much less to the future.

When we weren't immersed in long discussions around the

kitchen table in Kenny's New Rochelle home, we took trips to popular jazz clubs in Harlem. One evening, an old family friend, Marion Logan, asked me to stop by to meet Nat King Cole's daughter, Natalie. Marion had been trying to connect us since she thought that we had so much in common. I arrived with Joe, Linda, and Kenny an hour before we would have to leave to go up to a club in Harlem. Natalie was attending a college in Massachusetts and had come to New York City with a friend from school for a few days. I liked her enough to suggest that she accompany us to hear some music. Natalie was ready to go but then we all seemed to realize at once that her friend, who was white, might not feel comfortable clubbing in Harlem. This was the height of the black power era, and we were heavy into establishing our separate identity. Blacks and whites did not socialize together in our circles. The friend offered to stay behind at the Logans' house so that the five of us could go out and not have to worry about her. Selfishly, we did as she suggested.

When vacation ended, Joe and Kenny returned to Washington. Linda and I traveled twice a month to spend weekends with our men. Occasionally, they visited us in New York as well. I was surprised at how quickly things had heated up between Joe and me; Joe was receptive, and I was in need of love and reassurance. We were so good together. Our conversations were free and easy. Our thirst for politics and each other was insatiable. Since we only saw each other on weekends, there were few realities that we had to deal with. Life seemed wonderfully serene. I was delighted when two months after my divorce from Michael was final, Joe asked me to marry him. This time there were no doubts. I wanted desperately to be married to this man.

We told my parents of our plans, which had been neatly programmed for the next ten years: After we married, I would move to Washington, D.C., and work. Joe would complete his last year at Howard and then we would move to New York City so that we could both study at Columbia University. Joe planned to go to medical school while I attended their school of nursing. Once licensed, we would be off to the east coast of Africa to live and work.

My mother and father took the news very differently. They both liked Joe, but worried about the timing. Dad was the first to give in, but then he was always quick to think that marriage held the secret to success. It had certainly worked in his case.

Mom, the more practical of the two when it came to marriage, pleaded with us to wait. She even suggested that we live together. Dad was already somewhat appalled that we were sexually active. In his eyes, living together took the whole thing a little too far, so he joined Joe and me in pushing Mom to accept our plans.

But Mom remained reserved and cautious. She was opposed to my getting married again until Joe and I got to know each other better. She pointed out the flaws in our plans. We remained insistent. Joe wanted me to come to Howard as his wife, and I was flattered. With the blessing of one parent and the resignation of the other, we decided we would be married on Christmas Eve.

Three months before our wedding, I began to make my dress. I was working part-time at Krammer's Fabric Store in downtown Stamford, and the Krammers told me that the materials for my dress would be their wedding present. I had great fun learning about different fabrics, carefully selecting a luxurious white satin blend, and working on the dress each evening with love and devotion. It had to be perfect; I paid as much attention to detail as a servant in preparation for a royal ceremony.

On Christmas Eve, I wrapped my head in four yards of African fabric, slipped into my carefully constructed short, sleeveless wedding dress, and headed to the church to take my place beside my man with a mission. I was deliriously happy and very much in love.

For the first time in years, both of my brothers were home and my entire family was together. Grandma, Uncle Chuck, Aunt Brenda, and my cousins Rhoda, Kirk, and Chuckie met us at my grandmother's church in Brooklyn for the intimate service, with a big reception planned for after the holidays. I couldn't believe that I was being given another chance for marital bliss, and with such a wonderful man. At the age of nineteen, I said marriage vows for the second time.

Grandma had prepared a special celebratory dinner. With the family gathered in the dining room around the massive oblong table, Dad led us in prayer. There was, indeed, much to be thankful for. Smiling broadly, I sat across the table from my older brother. It was so good to see him at the dinner table. I was so into the high of the moment that I found it impossible to wait for Christmas morning to give Jackie his gift, so with everyone still gathered at the dining table, I presented him with his present.

I'll never forget how his eyes lit up as he pulled the brown leather vest, lined in paisley, out of the box. "I made it for you!" I blurted out, beaming. I was terribly proud of having made Jackie's vest, a difficult project. Jackie read the label, "Made especially for you by Sharon," stood up, and pulled the vest on. He looked good.

Jackie stood and stretched across the dining room table, angling his husky strong body toward me, and to my surprise, smacked a kiss dead on my lips. He kept his vest on all evening.

Just seeing my once-troubled, always edgy brother sitting relaxed, responsive, and in control was the best gift any of us could have received for Christmas. Self-confidence was evident in the way he talked, held his shoulders, let people back into his life, shared in conversation, and laughed. His eyes still looked a little haunted, but we couldn't help but feel optimistic.

I was determined to make this Christmas as different as it could be and I had wanted to find a special way to thank my family for their support over the past year. Personalized handmade gifts were my way to do it. I carefully selected patterns for outfits that reflected each family member and by Christmas morning my gifts were wrapped and placed under the tree as if they were store-bought: a long, bright, printed velvet skirt for Mom; a red dress with silver trim for Grandma; a green velvet monogrammed bathrobe for Joe, and a blue corduroy one-piece jumpsuit with a zipper up the front for Dad.

I snuggled contentedly up next to my new husband, watching everyone's reaction. Mom, Grandma, and Joe loved their gifts. I held my breath as my father pulled his jumpsuit out of the box. I knew he would tell me that he loved the present even if he really didn't, so I watched him closely, hoping his facial expression would be honest. His beautiful grin lit up the room.

"You made this?" he said, sounding surprised and impressed. Dad jumped right up and went to the bathroom to try on the sky blue corduroy suit. He prepared the pancakes that morning in his suit and wore it routinely ever after to cut the grass or lounge around the house. After breakfast, Dad led us in assembling the new stereo system he had purchased for Mom. Later, as I was in the process of wrapping presents for our cousins and Aretha Franklin's "Amazing Grace" was blasting through the house, I managed to cut the speaker wires. The music stopped dead and my brothers scrambled around the room trying to find out what had happened. I picked up the present I had just wrapped and screamed when I saw the cut wires. I burst into tears and the men gave me no mercy, teasing me the whole time they spliced the wires back together. But my tears and their laughter helped disperse the emotions that we were all feeling. I had come to accept each day as it came and knew that there were no guarantees. I was thankful for this blessed Christmas Day.

Married less than a week, Joe and I drove back to Washington, where he had rented an efficiency apartment in a three-family house. Joe had agreed to be the resident manager, so instead of fifty dollars a month, we paid forty. Joe rose at five each morning to light the ancient gas furnace housed in a small utility room about ten feet from our bed. The only thing separating us from that monster was a cloth curtain we hung over the doorway. The sound of the pilot light igniting was the signal that we'd have hot water in one hour.

I had fun decorating; I made a black fake fur bedspread, black-and-white printed curtains, and red throw pillows. There was a hallway that led from the combination living room and bedroom to the kitchen, and Joe had the strange notion of painting it a bright orange. But it did lighten the otherwise dark passageway.

The apartment had a large kitchen and a glass-paneled door that led out to the backyard.

This was my first experience living in an urban area. I had visions of a backyard with a flower garden and grass, even though the other backyards in the neighborhood were barren; I just assumed no one had made the effort. I had helped my mom maintain gardens at our Stamford house for years; surely, I thought, I could transform this small plot into something pleasant.

In early spring Joe helped me turn over the neglected dirt. We added fertilizer and proceeded to plant seeds. I was delighted when the first signs of grass began to appear. But I hadn't reckoned on the anger of the neighbor's dog; I had invaded his territory and restricted his mobility. He knocked over my barrier and trampled the tiny seedlings as if he knew that they were the enemy. The big dog and I tried to coexist, but eventually I gave in to the dog's proprietary rights, and relinquished the yard.

I had few complaints about my life. Joe was a loving husband and our lives seemed to be on track. Joe attended classes during the day and I found a job as a unit clerk in our neighborhood health care center at five thousand dollars a year. Combined with Joe's part-time work at the telephone company, we managed.

About the time we were feeling settled into our routine, my parents said they were coming to Washington on business and invited us out for dinner. Our budget didn't allow for entertainment or restaurants, so this was a double treat. We spent the weekend cleaning the apartment. Joe expressed concern that my father might not approve of the apartment or the neighborhood. I tried to reassure him that Dad knew our circumstances were temporary, and befitting of college students. Joe continued to be uneasy.

On the day my folks were to arrive, the Washington skies opened up, flooding parts of the city. I ran home, panicked, at lunchtime to survey the damage, but Joe had beaten me home. He was standing in the middle of the living room, water around his ankles, shaking his head.

We waded through the apartment picking up anything that could get damaged by the water and putting it on the bed, where the cat had taken refuge. There was nothing else to do but to wait it out. Eventually, the water would drain out of the house through the back door.

At six o'clock my parents pulled up in front in a long black limousine. Talk about embarrassing contrasts. I felt Joe's anguish but trusted my parents' ability to handle our circumstances. I smiled reassuringly at the man I loved and we headed to the limo hand in hand. We greeted my parents, explained our predicament, and Dad said, "Pack some clothes. We'll arrange for you to spend the night at our hotel."

The weekend with my parents was such fun! By the time they dropped us off at our apartment on Sunday afternoon the water had drained and we were able to show them around. Joe didn't mention until years later how embarrassed he was by the whole thing. All I knew then was that not long afterward, the edginess I noticed in Joe had deepened to a moody, silent depression. I tried to find out why, but at first Joe evaded my questions. I kept pressing, and finally Joe confessed that he had been expelled from Howard University. To my shock, he went on to admit that he had not been attending classes for the past year and had been warned at the end of the fall semester.

Once again I felt married to a lie. When I pushed him for an answer as to how he could have deceived me for so long, he said he had lost touch with his goals. There was no more SNCC. There was no central organization to take its place. The Black Panthers were out of control. He talked of missing the camaraderie and support from other members of SNCC and described a feeling of stepping off a treadmill before it came to a full stop. To cover the emptiness, he had locked himself into the militancy of the late sixties, which he ultimately found empty. Our love and marriage had revived him for a while, but the lie he was living finally caught up to him. The facade of strength, confidence, and achievement he had presented so long almost convinced him that his life was on target. The expulsion letter from Howard had shocked him back into reality.

As I listened to Joe, I felt a mixture of emotions that included

disappointment. I tried to mask my feelings and remain supportive, but my mother's warnings kept flashing through my mind:
"Get to know each other," she had said over and over.

"I'll be back in school by next semester," Joe promised. "I still
want to go to Columbia's medical school. In fact, there's no reason
to tell anyone. Especially our parents."

I didn't want to lie, but I mulled it over and reluctantly agreed
to keep his secret. I made only one condition. I wanted us to meet
with someone in the medical community who could guide us. The
first person who came to my mind was Dr. George Lythcott.

An associate dean at Columbia University College of Medicine,
Dr. Lythcott was a family friend and our first pediatrician. I hadn't
seen him in a few years, but I remembered his warmth and compassion. If he could comfort me at three when I had fallen off the
swing and broken my nose, surely he could handle this situation, I
thought. Maybe not the greatest logic, but it made me feel better,
and I thought Joe would be motivated by just meeting Dr.
Lythcott.

I called Dr. Lythcott's office, made an appointment, and two
weeks later introduced the two men and sat quietly as they talked.

The doctor encouraged Joe to look on the expulsion as a set-
back not a failure, and told him he needed to get back in school
as soon as possible. "If you can turn that situation around," he said,
"admission to medical school is certainly still within the realm of
possibility."

He offered his continued support and told Joe of Columbia
University's commitment to increasing minority enrollment in the
medical school. Joe was smiling and talking for the first time in
weeks.

Before we left, Dr. Lythcott said, "Sharon, what are your plans?"

"I want to go to nursing school."

"You should, and you should move right ahead on it. Keep in
mind it could take Joe two years to turn things around. Why not
look into the nursing schools in Washington? You can always go to
Columbia for graduate school."

We left Dr. Lythcott's office, and returned to Washington

thoughtful. We proceeded with our lives. Joe got a job in the poison control office at Children's Hospital. I applied to two nursing schools in the area, Federal City College and Howard University. But we were bandaging an open wound that really required sutures.

A few months later, I received notification that I had been accepted at both programs I applied to. I chose Howard University College of Nursing and enrolled in the summer of 1969. As the fall semester began, the campus came to life, and so did my feelings, swelling with a sense of power and control. I had been on campus before but only as Joe's wife. Now I belonged. I was surrounded by black people from all over the world. The administration was black. Most of my professors were black. It was so different from the feelings of alienation I felt growing up in all-white environments. It was also very different from the social experience with Jack & Jill. I felt a constant thrill as I moved from the science building at the base of the hill, to the School of Fine Arts, and back down the hill to the College of Medicine for anatomy and physiology. In my classes, I kept pace with hundreds of budding young doctors, scientists, writers, and even mathematicians, all black. I swelled with pride and nearly burst with expectation and possibility. I became thirsty for knowledge, eager for experience, and ready to achieve.

Part of my enthusiasm undoubtedly stemmed from the male population. The campus was pregnant with distractions; I had never seen so many handsome black men in one place in my life. I was actually relieved that I was married or I would have been as confused as my unmarried classmates—there were entirely too many possibilities.

During the day I attended classes and worked part-time at the National Business League. At night, I returned home to a man whom I still loved but could no longer communicate with. Joe had made two attempts to reenroll at Howard, but he couldn't negotiate the structure or the demands of the classroom. It seemed that his life, devoid of the political activism of his early college years, had no direction.

Watching my husband was like looking at a mirror image of my former self, and I felt as if I was going into partnership with death. At school, I felt free, creative, and alive. At home, I felt like a caged animal, afraid to expose my growing passion for life for fear that it would further threaten my lost husband. We stayed together physically, but grew further and further apart emotionally each day.

The highlight of that period was the birth of my godson, Reginald Richter. His mother, Susan Neal, and I were classmates and close friends. I adored Reggie and kept him with me many nights so that his mother could work. It's hard to believe Reggie's in law school now. Reggie's presence in my life helped me through a difficult time in my marriage.

I had thought I could escape into marriage, and when it didn't work, I chose flight once again. I told Joe that we had to separate. I found out that it wasn't going to be that easy.

"Hey, sis, what's up?" Jackie asked on the phone, sounding surprised to hear from me.

"I'm coming home tomorrow night and I need to talk with you. I'm leaving Joe."

"Why?" my brother wanted to know.

"I'm too tired to talk now, Jackie. I need to sit down with you. Will you be home tomorrow evening?" I asked, suddenly feeling the magnitude of the burden.

"I have a meeting about the concert Daytop is having at the house in two weeks. I'll be home around ten. Wait up for me."

"Thanks, Jackie. I'll see you tomorrow." Just putting the phone back into the cradle was a chore. I could barely undress to get into bed. I pulled the covers up around me and folded my body around my pillow. Thank God I have Jackie to talk to, I thought. He would know what to do, maybe even intervene for me. I was still very much in love with Joe.

Joe and I talked by phone later that evening. He told me that he wanted our marriage, that it made a difference. He said he couldn't bear being separated from me, and that he would get his life back on track if I would come home. He said something about how supportive I had been with my brother. How could I explain to him that I expected more from my husband than my brother? I loved him, but I needed him to fight back for himself. I told him as much.

"Strength, Joe. I need to see some strength. You keep showing me weakness."

"Yes, but everyone needs support. Remember the time we searched the local hangouts looking for Jackie?"

I remembered that evening all too well. My parents were frantic. They hadn't heard from Jackie in over a month. They had tried to locate him by going to the pool hall on West Main Street and calling a few of his friends, but their attempts were fruitless. Out of desperation they asked me to try and find out something. Joe and I went to the same pool hall; I knew some of the boys there from high school. They were secretive, but finally suggested that I try a nearby apartment building.

We went to the run-down building, knocked on the door of the apartment we had been sent to. A man answered, said Jackie wasn't there, but if he saw him he would let him know I was looking for him. We visited a few more spots, leaving messages wherever we went. We didn't find Jackie, but he called within twenty-four hours.

Just listening to Joe bring all this up again was exhausting. My only peace was remembering that I was going to Connecticut the next day to be with my dad and talk to my brother. I knew that Mom was in Massachusetts for the weekend attending a group relations conference.

As I drifted off to sleep I kept asking myself: Why me? Why Joe? Why twice in my lifetime? I know what people mean when they say that they're heartsick. It seemed like a dull pain radiated from my heart and traveled throughout my body.

The four-hour train ride from Washington to New York gave me time to think, but as the train pulled into Pennsylvania Station I still had no answers. My movements were mechanical. I followed the crowd out of the building. Dad was parked right in front of the train station, and I perked up at the sight of the familiar car.

Dad's hair was now almost completely white. He looked much older than his fifty-two years. He was talking to his new attorney, Marty Edelman, and I was glad there was going to be a third person in the car. Dad knew that Joe and I were having marital problems, but I didn't want to discuss the state of my marriage in the car with Marty. I needed to talk with Jackie first.

I climbed into the front seat next to my father and reached over to give him a kiss. It was good to see him. Dad made the introductions. Marty was a young lawyer, about thirty. I remembered Jesse Jackson had introduced them.

Dad wanted to know about school. I came alive. I was so happy at Howard, taking a chemistry course in summer school and for the first time understanding the material. I needed at least a C to begin my clinical rotations in the fall, and I was aching to get into the hospital.

Dad filled Marty in on the transformation that had occurred since I'd been at Howard. He talked of my growing confidence and lust for life. "It's hard to believe that this is the same young woman we sent off to Washington two years ago."

We talked about Mom, Jackie, and David. My father's face lit up. Dad told me he and Jackie had recently appeared together on a radio show, talking about their evolving relationship and Jackie's drug addiction. Dad said that Jackie was enjoying his new role as a member of the Daytop staff, that he was speaking to community, church, and youth groups in the New Haven area. He also ran a rehabilitation group. Occasionally, he was asked to speak to groups in New York. Dad said that Jackie had even testified before a U.S. Senate Subcommittee to Investigate Juvenile Delinquency.

I admired my brother's courage. I was glad that he was finding a way to release his own pain and help others at the same time. But I couldn't help wondering how Dad was really handling Jackie's revelations. On the surface anyway my father seemed only pleased that he and Jackie were finally communicating.

Jackie had also been reunited with his daughter. Sonya was an expressive five-year-old eager to be in her father's presence. The wounds between Jackie and her grandfather were healed, allowing him free access to his child.

Dad was equally as animated discussing David's coming home from college. He had completed his freshman year at Stanford University and had just driven across country in his yellow MG. David and Dad had similar temperaments and had always been close. Dad told me that David would be waiting for us when we got home. The three of us were going to dinner at Manero's, our favorite family steak restaurant in Greenwich.

We dropped Marty off in Rye and then continued the twenty or so miles to Stamford. When we pulled up into our driveway, my skinny brother David was waiting on the front steps. I hugged him, realizing that he had sprouted taller still by another few inches, and had also grown a mustache.

David did most of the talking at dinner. He is such a vivid storyteller. He was in the midst of a story when we heard a small voice:

"Are you really Jackie Robinson?" A boy of about eight or nine had approached our table, unnoticed until our attention was drawn by his innocent interruption. He was clutching a napkin and a pen in his hand. Dad had the greatest amount of patience with children. If an adult interrupted a family dinner he could be abrupt, requiring that the autograph seeker not only have a pen but that the pen be cocked and ready to write.

"Yes, I am," Dad responded with a smile.

"May I have your autograph?" the boy wanted to know.

"What is your name?" Dad liked to personalize autographs. "It was nice meeting you, Adam—keep those grades up," he added shaking the boy's hand. We watched as the boy returned to his table, flashing his signed napkin and white teeth.

We returned home around nine. David walked across the street to visit a friend. Jackie was still out and I was tired, so I put a note on his pillow telling him to wake me when he got home. I said good night to Dad and headed for bed. Dr. Allen, Candy's father, was picking me up at 6 A.M. so that we could drive to Cambridge for Candy's graduation from Harvard.

I was sound asleep when the doorbell rang. I jumped out of bed without glancing at the clock. I figured that either my brother had forgotten his key or I had overslept and it was Dr. Allen coming to pick me up. I ran to the front door, opened it, and found myself face-to-face with a uniformed policeman.

The officer mumbled something about my brother having been in an accident. His speech was barely audible.

"Just a minute," I said, not taking the time to ask him which of my brothers he was referring to. I turned and saw my father standing behind me. I checked Jackie's room first. His bed hadn't been slept in. The note that I had written to him lay untouched on the pillow. I headed to David's room and called to him to get up quickly, saying that we had to get to the hospital because Jackie had been hurt.

I then dashed back to the door to find out from the policeman where they had taken Jackie. The first thing I noticed was that my father had not moved from the spot where I had left him. I looked from my father to the policeman, sensing that something was very wrong. Jackie's condition must be serious. The police officer must have given my father more information while I was down the hall.

"I'm sorry, Mr. Robinson." I had no trouble hearing the man that time. Sorry about what? I wanted to say. I looked into my father's ashen face.

"Let's go," I said, defiantly.

"There's no need to rush," Dad replied without moving. "Jackie's dead."

14

The Baptism

I was haunted by the image of being the son of a father who was a great man. So, when I found I couldn't deal with him as a man and found that my father couldn't identify with me as his son, I stopped trying to find a man who wasn't there. I tried to eliminate the desire that I thought would never be fulfilled. Daytop helped me through discipline to find the father I had lost. In the process I lied, cheated, robbed, and dealt with prostitutes. After I tried marijuana I reached out for bigger and better thrills, egged on by my friends who called me square for being afraid. At Daytop I found not only myself but love. My family closed ranks to help me in every way possible. My father was always in my corner. I didn't always recognize that and I didn't always call on him, but he was always there.

Jackie Robinson Jr., U.S. Senate Subcommittee hearings,
October 30, 1970

"Sharon, we will have to drive to Massachusetts and get to your mother before the press does. David, call Dr. Allen and ask him to come over." Dad's voice was surprisingly steady. He was giving clear directions. Nobody cried.

I was barely able to move, too numb to feel. Jackie had survived Vietnam. Graduated from a drug treatment program. He had just started to live. You can't die at twenty-four. It must be a mistake. Besides, we had planned to talk. I needed his advice, counted on him to see me through my crisis with Joe. I felt consumed with anger. The police always lie! But the building rage died as quickly as it came. The news began to sink in. All I could think of was my poor mother. What were we going to tell her?

Dad divided up the tasks. David volunteered to go to the hospital to identify the body. Dr. Allen arrived and brought over a sedative for my parents if they needed it. Dad and I headed north on the Merritt Parkway trying to get to Mom before daybreak, and the press.

Dad and I really didn't understand what they did at these group relations conferences, yet we made no secret of the fact that we didn't approve. They took Mom away for days at a time and she returned worn out. We voiced our criticisms without making any effort to find out why she went. With Dad's health problems, he was slowing down, and becoming even more dependent on my mother. In fact, it seemed that they had switched roles, with my mother often away on business and my father awaiting her return each time. It was not only Dad's health that was a problem, his pride was hurting. Ever since he had resigned from Chock Full O'Nuts his income had been less predictable and the truth was that they needed the two incomes.

Dad and I drove in silence on the same highway where my brother had died earlier that morning. I stared out the window trying to keep my thoughts away from the crash. Maybe he really was gone, I told myself.

I tried to remember something good. All I could re-create was the time that Mom and I came home from my ballet class to find our driveway filled with fire trucks. Mom knew without being told that it had something to do with Jackie. Jackie, who was nine, had a blank look on his face as the fire chief told the story of the boys trespassing and starting a fire in the reservoir.

Jackie was quick to tell his side. He gave the old Boy Scout story, the one about rubbing two sticks together then resorting to matches when friction didn't do the job. After all, they were only trying to build a small campfire. Setting the woods on fire was an accident.

Jackie was always the innocent bystander. One time he had a rather frail friend over to visit. The boy had come to play with

Jackie for the first time. Somehow, Jackie shot him in the head with his BB gun. The boy wasn't hurt, but Mom had some time trying to explain it to the boy's parents.

Finally a happy image came to mind. In May 1970, my parents had a picnic for the Daytop staff and residents. About fifty people came. Though we'd had lots of events on our lawn over the years, this was the most special. I was struck by how loving Jackie was toward the other members, the staff, and to us. As the day came to a close each person came up to my mother and father to thank them. Jackie was last. He reached out and grabbed Mom, hugging her lovingly. Then he got to Dad. My father, remembering how his earlier efforts to hug Jackie had been rejected, reached out to shake his son's hand. Jackie brushed Dad's hand aside, pulled his father to him, and hugged him tightly.

Dad later wrote in his autobiography, "That single moment paid for every bit of sacrifice, every bit of anguish, I had ever undergone. I had my son back."

Now he had been taken away again and I couldn't help but wonder why: Why, Jackie? Were you driving too fast? Had you been drinking? Did you have a fight with your girlfriend or did you just fall asleep at the wheel? I caught myself in an old pattern. I had no reason to think it was Jackie's fault.

In no time at all it seemed, Dad pulled into the driveway of Mount Holyoke College. The moment we dreaded had come too fast. The campus was much too peaceful. The sun, if it could rise at all on a day like this, had not yet burned off the low mists.

We stopped at the guard's office and found out Mom's room number. We headed to the building. We hadn't thought what to say. My heart was racing. Dad still hadn't said a word. We walked in silence and didn't touch. I knocked on the door. Mom called out through the closed door.

"It's Sharon, Mom."

"Sharon!" I heard her cry out, panicked. She swung the door open. Her eyes were wild, but settled on our faces.

Dad spoke: "We lost him."

Mom collapsed in our arms.

★   ★   ★

Jackie's face was on the cover of the *New York Times* and the *Stamford Advocate* the next morning. He had been driving David's MG, fallen asleep at the wheel, crashed into a fence, and then into an abutment on the Merritt Parkway. He had been working long hours on the jazz concert, scheduled for ten days later, June 27, 1971, to benefit Daytop.

His funeral was held at Antioch Baptist Church in Brooklyn. David spoke for the family. He had written Jackie a prose poem entitled "The Baptism":

> And he climbed high on the cliffs above the sea and stripped bare his shoulders and raised his arms to the water, crying: "I am a man. I live and breathe and bleed as a man. Give me my freedom so that I might dance naked in the moonlight and laugh with the stars as they play amongst the darkness in the sky and roll in the grass and drink the warmth of the sun and feel it sweet within my body. Give me my freedom so that I might fly."
>
> But the armies of the sea continued to war with the beach and the wind raced through the giants of stones which guard the coast and its howl mocked its cries and the man fell to his knees and wept. Then he rose and journeyed down the mountain to the valley and came upon a village. When the people saw him they scorned him for his naked shoulders and wild eyes and again he cried: "I am a man and I seek the means of my freedom." But the people laughed at him, saying, "We see no chains on your arms, no weight on your feet. Go! You are free. Fly! Fly! Fly!" And they called him mad and drove him from their village. His soul wept, for it knew the weight of chains, and tears fell like tiny stones into the well of his loneliness, and his heart was empty as a giant hall is empty after a feast.
>
> And the man journeyed on until he came to the banks of a stream, and his eyes, red as the gladiator's sword, strained, for he saw an image dance across the stillness of that water and

he recognized the figure though his eyes were now sunken with hunger and skin drawn tight around his body and he stood fixed above the water's edge and began to weep, not from sorrow but from joy, for he saw beauty in the water and he removed his clothing and stood naked before the world and he rose to his full height and smiled as the sun kissed his body and he moved to meet with the figure in the water and the stream made love to his body, and his soul cried with the ecstasy of being one, and he sent the water flying up like a shower of diamonds to the sky, and he laughed for he felt the strength of the stream flowing through his veins, and he cried: "I am a man" and was heard above the roar of the sea and the howl of the wind, and he was free.

The next week was filled with a flurry of activity. We had to go through with the concert, had to do it for Jackie. He had worked so hard to make it a success. But there was still much to be done.

Friends and relatives filled our house, helping with the last-minute preparations. We stayed up late each night making signs, planning menus, ordering Porta-Johns. The night before the concert, Twanda Bowers, Natalie Dickerson, Linda, and a few of my other girlfriends hovered in a corner of the living room making signs and discussing Jesse Jackson as if he were a rock star, African prince, or Greek god:

"I guess he's about six two."

"But, girl, that hair!"

"He's coming with Roberta." Jackie had invited Jesse Jackson and Roberta Flack.

Twanda giggled as if she knew something. "That doesn't matter, I'll be close enough to touch him."

"He'll probably have on one of his dashikis."

Enough, I thought. What was so great about Jesse Jackson? I wanted to know. I'd heard Dad speak of him a few times, but from the way the girls were talking I was obviously missing something. I was embarrassed to admit that I didn't know much about him. If they had said Stokely Carmichael, Huey P., or Rap Brown I'd have been excited, too. But Jesse Jackson from Chicago? I moved to another room, tired of the girls' silly chatter.

I made a purple tie-dyed outfit for the afternoon. It had a long wrap skirt and a short midriff top and I wore no shoes. I no longer wore my hair in a nine-inch afro and had it cut down to its curly roots. By six-thirty the morning of the concert, I was up and dressed. The volunteers were due to arrive at eight, and the gate would open at ten.

At nine-thirty I was standing at the top of the hill in our back-yard between Dr. Allen and Uncle Chuck. It was a glorious, cloud-less day, an answer to our prayers. But grief has a way of hitting you like a bolt of lightning. It comes and goes without warning. This was one of those moments. Tears just starting pouring down my face. Uncle Chuck took me in his arms, saying that he understood.

Why couldn't he have lived to see the fruits of his labor? There were so many unanswered questions. "Don't let your mother see you crying," Uncle Chuck whispered softly in my ear.

I straightened up and took a deep breath. He was right. If I started the day in tears, I might not make it through.

People began to arrive, carrying picnic baskets, blankets, straw hats, and coolers. Grandma Isum was in charge of the kitchen. Dad directed the parking of cars and greeted people as they arrived. And Mom was directing the whole production.

Uncle Chuck and I wandered through the lawns welcoming our guests. Miss Flack's musicians arrived first. Then she arrived in a long black limousine. Some of the younger jazz musicians warmed up the audience, setting the tone for "An Afternoon of Jazz."

I was so caught up in the mood sitting on top of my favorite boulder that I hadn't realized that Jesse Jackson had arrived. My attention was drawn to a group of seven or so who were slowly making their way toward the stage. A rush of energy passed through the crowd. Excitement was building. From the distance it was difficult to distinguish all of the members of the group, but I spotted Dad and Kenny Williams. A tall, dashiki-clad man kept bending to shake the outstretched hands. I realized that it had to

be Jesse Jackson. The group finally reached the stage. The crowd
was silent. Dad stepped up to the microphone, thanked the people
for coming, and then introduced Reverend Jackson, the "Country
Preacher."

The man who had been a stranger to me was obviously not a
stranger to the rest of the cheering audience. As he spoke I made
my way to the front of the crowd. Dad was reclining on the grass
right in front of the stage and he welcomed me with a warm smile
and outstretched arms. I sat motionless, nestled in his arms. Jesse
talked about all that Jackie had overcome. The message was upbeat,
hopeful. This was not a time to mourn. It was a time to reflect,
rejoice, appreciate all that Jackie had accomplished. Still, the anger
inside me remained.

"Don't measure Jackie's life only by the day that he was born
and the day he died—the length of the journey matters less than
the deeds he accomplished along the way . . ." Jackson's voice was
strong, reaching the crescendo characteristic of a preacher about to
conclude his sermon. Only this was not a church and it was not
the choir who provided the transition. I recognized the voice
immediately as Roberta Flack's: "Old Pharaoh, let my people
go . . ." Roberta came up from behind the stage holding her own
microphone. Jesse's voice faded as Roberta's rose, "Pharaoh, let my
people go . . ."

I had been so shocked by the tragedy of Jackie's death that I
hadn't been able to see any light. Now though, I allowed myself to
hope that maybe he hadn't died in vain. I thought of all the young
people, parents, clergy, and counselors he had reached with his
antidrug message. Maybe their lives were now different as a result
of his honesty. I thought of the parents who were suffering alone
until they were touched by my brother. Was it possible that they
were able to cope better with their children? I wanted to freeze the
moment. A familiar voice filtered into my semiconscious state:
"This must be your daughter."

Jesse Jackson squatted down to our level and talked softly with
my father while Roberta sang on. I listened in; Jesse told Dad that
he wanted to talk with the family before he left. The three of us

rose and ascended the hillside. I went off to find David. Dad rounded up Mom and Grandma. We met in Mom and Dad's bedroom.

When Jesse asked us to join hands so that we could pray, my mother and I erupted in anger. We demanded an explanation: Why had God taken Jackie just as he was beginning to live? Jackson didn't seem surprised or thrown by our reaction to his suggestion of prayer. He skillfully calmed our hysteria and assured us that even if we could not see it at the moment, someday it would make sense. I'm not sure who was most grateful for his intervention. My suspicion is that it was Dad.

We finally held hands and bowed our heads. Jesse prayed. The private pain of one of us became a collective hurt, bringing all of us closer.

15

Bread from Heaven

Shortly after Jackie's funeral, Mom and Dad went back to work. David returned to Stanford, and Joe and I headed home with our marriage and my chemistry course to deal with. The crisis had brought Joe and me closer. I learned more about Joe's disappointment in himself. We even talked of having a baby.

For the next six weeks, I concentrated on passing chemistry, studying long hours until the material made sense. My final grade was only a C but I treated it like an A. I felt invincible.

Over the summer, I made frequent trips home. My telephone calls were not adequate to determine my parents' state of mind. I was worried. The loss of Jackie was the most traumatic and tragic moment in my parents' life and I wanted them to know how much I loved them. On my visits, Mom seemed withdrawn and Dad so much slower and older.

On one visit in particular, I knew that something was terribly wrong when Dad picked me up at the train station and hardly talked all the way home. Dinner was void of its usual discussion and after the meal, Mom headed to her bedroom and Dad pulled up a chair in front of the television. I cleaned up the kitchen and then went off to my bedroom. Around eight, I ventured out of my room in search of a snack. The house was silent. I turned on the hallway lights and headed toward the kitchen, assuming that my father had gone to bed. Puzzled by the unhealthy stillness, I moved cautiously.

As I neared the entrance to the living room I stopped, startled by the sound of muffled sobs. I stood still listening for a minute trying to identify the source. I looked into the living room. There was a shadowy figure silhouetted by the light coming into the room from a full moon. As my eyes adjusted, I realized that the slumped body sitting on the couch was my father. Dad was sitting alone in the darkness crying.

"Dad? Dad?" I called out softly, unaccustomed to this raw display of emotion from my father. "Dad, is that you?"

I stepped down into the living room, walking slowly toward my father wondering if I was doing the right thing. Was I intruding in a private moment? Should I go back to my room and pretend not to have witnessed my father crying?

My heart propelled my feet forward in spite of the reservations. Dad was an emotional rock. I couldn't ever remember seeing him cry. I took the last five steps still not sure of what I would say once I reached him or how to help him. I sat on the arm of the couch and hugged my father.

"Dad, why are you crying?" I asked in a choked voice.

"First Mr. Rickey and my mother, then your brother." Dad's voice trembled as he spoke.

It was times like this that made me realize that my father may have seemed like our center, but my mother was our true foundation. She was the one we rallied behind and depended upon. We couldn't afford to lose her. Chills began to creep up inside of me. I had certainly contributed to my mother's unhappiness and given her little indication of how important she was to my life. Publicly and privately, Dad never failed to appreciate how essential my mother was to all of us. But he had also complained often about her career, and neither of us had made any attempt to understand why it was so important to her. I should have been the first to understand her passion for work, but I was too focused on my own needs.

I kissed my father on the cheek, squeezed his shoulders, which for the first time didn't seem so broad, got up and left the room. It was not my comfort that Dad needed.

I headed straight to the master suite, took a deep breath, and knocked on the door. I knew that it was unfair to my mother to burden her with our needs at this time. She wanted time by herself to work through her grief. We had always been so demanding of my mother's support, rarely considering what her needs might be. But Dad needed her once again, and more so than ever, and I prayed that she would have the strength to open herself to him.

I knocked again on my parents' bedroom door. After a brief pause, I heard her voice. "Come in."

I opened the door and gingerly approached. Mom was sitting up in her bed reading.

"Mom, Dad is crying," I blurted out and continued without taking a breath. The startled expression on my mom's face gave me immediate confidence in her reaction. My heart stopped racing.

"Sharon, where is he?" Her voice was strong and warm at the same time.

"Thanks for coming to get me," Mom said as she pulled on her robe and hurried to her husband.

Gradually, my visits home became less stressful. Dad was busy with a number of entrepreneurial efforts, one of which was problems associated with Freedom National Bank. As chairman, Dad had to confront the president of the bank about some questionable loans. He was nervous and tense about the suggestion of an impropriety. Since white-owned banks had a tendency to deny loans to African-Americans, Freedom National Bank was an important institution for economic development in Harlem. Another of my father's ventures was a company called Seahost, which attempted to market frozen fish to the black community. It didn't last long.

Then there was investment in a line of women's beauty products along with Marian and Arthur Logan. The venture was not very successful. Boxes of the unsold products ended up in the Logans' basement.

At times, I thought my father a little too trusting for the business world. After ten successful years in corporate America, Dad's latest ventures into entrepreneurship had been less satisfying. I hoped that the construction company would give his self-esteem and finances a needed boost.

The Jackie Robinson Construction Company planned to get government contracts to build apartment complexes for low- and moderate-income families. With the advent of minority set-asides and my father's high visibility, they were well placed. While Dad was busy forming his company, Mom was building a career and reputation in the field of mental health as the director of nursing for the Connecticut Mental Health Center and assistant clinical professor at Yale University School of Nursing.

Even though both of my parents were occupied with work, Dad seemed to need Mom's presence more than ever. He demonstrated this need with subtle protests. There were times when my father would refuse to eat the dinner that Grandma had prepared until my mother got home from work. My mother, thinking that she had graduated beyond having to take care of a needy family, dragged herself home exhausted, often well after six, only to find that her diabetic husband had missed eating on schedule. Dad would make up some excuse, but it was obvious to the rest of the family that by holding out Dad was showing his displeasure over Mom's career.

The dependence masked my father's fears. There was no denying that his health had become a serious problem and he must have sensed that he would not live for much longer. A couple of times that fall, he was hospitalized and I was called home. Visits to see him were excruciating. The closer I would get to the hospital, the more my heart would pound and even breathing became difficult. We had just lost Jackie and I feared that Dad would follow too soon.

I would walk into my father's hospital room firing words in rapid succession, telling funny stories, describing in great detail my nursing instructors. Anything to keep at bay the topic of how serious my father's health problems really were. I became a master of avoidance. Within an hour of my arrival at my father's bedside, I was suggesting that Mom and I go out to dinner.

Dad was always very pleased to see me. I could also tell that he was grateful that I had come to relieve my mother. Just getting beyond the boundaries of the hospital was a relief. Once outside, Mom and I would focus on other things. One evening, Mom described her attempts to provide high-quality care to the community surrounding Yale and to also satisfy the residents who were suspicious of anyone attached to Yale. Once, an angry male, self-appointed delegation marched into a disciplinary hearing my mother held for one of her employees. They encircled the room standing at attention with their arms wrapped around their backs, and tried to intimidate with their cold stares and threatening statements. Mom held her ground. When her supervising physician, a white psychiatrist from Yale, attempted to defend Mom, two of the men held the doctor up by his collar, at which point my mother jumped up and confronted them and told them that their tactics were not going to work.

I laughed at my 125-pound mother "wolfing." But even the fact that I could readily visualize Mom taking on a group of angry men told me a lot about her character. My mother would never allow herself to be victimized.

Mom's stories about her work were almost as fascinating as her encapsulations of David's letters from Africa. He had left Stanford and was hitchhiking from Egypt to Kenya. Once, he traveled through the countryside in Kenya watching the sunset and counting elephants as he lay on bags of grain in the back of a pickup truck. When he arrived, he didn't speak any Swahili. He managed to communicate with greetings, simple directions, and when all else failed a smile, a look of amusement or surprise.

When David left on his travels, he promised to return in time for the fall semester. Midway through his trip he realized he couldn't leave. He wrote to Mom and Dad that leaving Africa now would be like walking out on a play after the first act. David had a big score to settle. At nineteen, he was in search of himself after years of being defined by a lily white private school.

On good days, David's news was upbeat, funny, insightful. Occasionally, though, a letter would arrive that would send Mom into a near panic thinking that her youngest child was losing his mind. The words were confused, messages vague, life drastic. We longed for his safe return, hoping that this adventure would calm the inner turmoil and help to satisfy his wanderlust.

Joe and I continued to live together, but the closeness we shared just after Jackie died did not last. We avoided talk of a future together.

In spite of my disappointment with Joe, I was not swayed from my goals. I emerged in the fall of 1971 with all my prerequisite courses out of the way and the credits to join my classmates in the nursing program. According to the college of nursing curriculum, we would now study in the classroom only three days a week and then spend two days a week on the hospital wards caring for patients. To mark this transition, the college planned a formal capping ceremony.

After weeks of anticipation and preparation, my classmates and I arrived at Rankin Chapel dressed for the first time in our Howard University student nurse uniforms, a starched, blue-and-white pinstriped dress with a round navy blue collar covered by a white apron that buttoned on either side, white stockings, and brand-new white oxford nursing shoes.

We assembled in the lower level of the chapel, lined up by height. There were about thirty members of the class of 1973; a fairly diverse group in terms of age, marital status, and even nationality. Our common linkage was our collective African descent and our desire and determination to become nurses.

Nervous with expectation, I clutched my white candle tightly as we proceeded in pairs up the stairs and into the stained-glass chapel. The room was packed. As my eyes adjusted to the dim lighting, I spotted my mother and father sitting in the middle section. Dad was at the end of the aisle.

When I applied to Howard I did so using my married name. Prior to the capping ceremony, I had remained determined to maintain my anonymity. To do so meant talking about my parents to my classmates and friends at school only in general terms and asking a few close friends not to disclose my secret. I lived off campus, held down a part-time job, and socialized mostly with students outside of nursing. So, for the first twelve months at Howard, I moved freely about the student body without fear of being singled out because of my parents' fame.

On this night of celebration, though, I no longer felt the need to hide. As I marched across the stage the night of the capping ceremonies I knew that by the end of the evening I would still be Sharon but I would also be Jackie Robinson's daughter. I felt a tremendous sense of relief to be able to equally embrace both.

My mother told me after the ceremony that on the way down to Washington my father acted as though he were going to the coronation of the queen. In retrospect, it was all the more important because it was the last of my milestones that my father would live to see.

After the formal part of the ceremony came to a close, my classmates and I scattered in search of family and friends. I rushed joyously into my parents' arms, happy and carefree as a five-year-old at her birthday party. Mom, Dad, and I joined the receiving line and waited our turn to greet the faculty. Although I pretended not to notice, I felt the stares, heard the whispers, and recognized the confusion. We were next in line.

"Dean Coles, I'd like you to meet my parents, Jack and Rachel Robinson." I spoke without taking my eyes off Dean Coles's face. She was known for being dramatic. I wondered how she would play this scene. A striking, elegant woman who stood nearly six feet tall, her eyes met my father's directly.

"I'm very pleased to meet you both," she said, remaining gracious and poised, and giving in only slightly to her delight at having a celebrity in her midst. As soon as the receiving line broke, Dean Coles approached with a photographer and our mutual good feeling was photographically preserved.

The excitement I felt as I embarked upon the clinical portion of the program continued throughout the semester. I loved being in the hospital and part of a team, my skills needed and valued. As the semester began to wind down I kept looking forward. Life was definitely on an upswing.

My father decided to take the family to Jamaica for the Christmas holidays. We had not celebrated Thanksgiving that year; Jackie's death was still too fresh in everyone's mind; and we hoped to avoid some of the sentiment associated with Christmas by spending the season in the warm sunshine.

Dad was finding it ever harder to disguise his health worries. The trip seemed to brighten his spirits though. Christmas Eve we had a quiet family dinner. Christmas morning we lounged around the grounds, walking the beaches, climbing the rocky cliffs, soaking in the sunshine, and being quietly reflective. Our spirits picked back up as December 25 was crossed off the calendar. My father suggested that we call home and tell Grandma Isum and Marian Logan to get on the next plane to Kingston.

Marian and her husband, Arthur, were more family than friends. The friendship dated back to my dad's baseball career. Marian was a nightclub singer who often spent winters singing in and around Miami, Florida. The Dodgers settled into the same area for spring training. With the hotels and public facilities segregated and only one Negro motel in the area, it is no wonder that Marian ended up in the same motel as Don Newcombe, Roy Campanella, and my father. There was many a night when Marian would come in from a gig and find the three men playing cards in the motel lobby. Years later Marian married Dr. Arthur C. Logan and gave up her singing career. The Logans and the Robinsons became the best of friends. Marian and Arthur's only child, Warren A. "Chip" Logan, was my parents' godson.

From the moment Marian and Zellee stepped off the six-seater plane in Port Antonio, laughter filled our days and nights.

"Never again!" Marian shouted from the steps of the plane, swinging her fur coat over one shoulder and hoisting her Gucci bag onto the other. She descended the steps in front of my grandmother, still muttering under her breath. Grandma was equally shaken, but considerably more subdued. She could only manage to mumble her gratitude for being included in the vacation. Apparently, the trip across the mountains had been a bit bumpy. They hadn't even noticed the beautiful countryside. Grandma prayed from the moment she got on the plane until it landed, while Marian drank "bubbly," as she affectionately referred to Champagne.

My father's doctor had prescribed a nightly cocktail of vodka and orange juice. Aunt Marian, happy to have him join her for cocktail hour, made a big production out of Dad's nightly cocktail. Dad didn't want anyone to get the wrong impression, so he would reluctantly accept his "medicine" and swallow the drink in one gulp as if it were some bad-tasting cough syrup. Marian laughed and teased, extolling the virtues of that six-ounce screwdriver until even he was giggling.

The next day we persuaded Dad to join us on the beach. Now, this was a first to beat all other firsts. My father had a fear of water and had never learned to swim. On all our earlier family vacations on islands with beautiful sandy beaches and crystal clear sea water, my father had kept his distance from the water. But on this trip, either he felt infallible or he sensed that this might be his last opportunity. Whatever the motivation, to our amazement Dad started to venture into the water. I stared, stunned, unable to move for a moment. I grabbed Dad's hand. Marian and Mom started jumping up and down cheering my father on. They acted like high school cheerleaders. David, who had returned from Africa before the holidays, navigated, demonstrating the depth of the water as he led the way. We slowly descended deeper and deeper into the sea. When the water reached Dad's waist, he tugged at my hand. We had gone far enough.

Our vacation in Jamaica passed quickly and its ending was bittersweet. It had been a long time since I had heard my mother and father laugh. Two days later, my father boarded the small jet with Marian and my grandmother. Mom, David, and I planned to stay for five more days. I hated seeing them leave. With Marian gone, the condo was much too quiet.

Dad called us when he got home. He called again the next day to say that his doctors wanted to hospitalize him immediately to try some new laser treatment on his eyes. I heard my mom say that we would leave Jamaica the next day. I reacted selfishly to the news of our shortened vacation.

"Why couldn't it wait a few more days?" I questioned my mother. Mom told David and me to pack. Dad needed us.

We arrived in New York the next day. Once we got there I, too, knew that it was the right decision. My father was anxious at the prospect of the experimental procedure to alleviate the loss of sight he had been experiencing. The vessels in his eyes had become enlarged and twisted, and the arteries narrowed. There was leakage of fluid from the blood vessels and it was beginning to accumulate on the retina.

My father was scheduled for the laser therapy the day after we got home. When the first treatment seemed to improve his vision, we all felt hopeful. Dad was discharged. Further treatments were not as successful, however. In fact, it caused more damage to the retina. My father was left blind in one eye.

16

Turned My Wailing into Dancing

You turned my wailing into dancing; you removed my
sackcloth and clothed me with joy.

Psalms 30:11

Just before we left for vacation in Jamaica, *Sport* magazine
announced that Jackie Robinson had been named "The Man of
the 25 Years in Sports." A luncheon in his honor marked the beginning of ten months of celebrating the twenty-fifth anniversary of
his entry into the major league, which included the Dodger's
retirement of Dad's number and culminated in the ceremony at
the World Series. It was quite a wonderful, happy time, beginning
with the morning of December 6 when a limousine drove us into
Manhattan to Mamma Leone's. It was one of my father's favorite
restaurants and he had brought us there many times. Dad stood tall
among the other giants being honored that day. Willie Mays,
Arnold Palmer, Gale Sayers, John Unitas, Rocky Marciano, and
Vince Lombardi were just a few names I recall.

As we walked into the lobby of the restaurant, my parents were
immediately swept up into the spotlight of reporters and cameras,
leaving Candy and me the freedom to explore the room. We were

actually in pursuit of Kareem Abdul-Jabbar. Cruising the room, we spotted him sitting off to the side talking with Bill Russell. The fearless twosome, Candy and I, headed toward them.

"I am Sharon Robinson and this is my friend Candy Allen." I reached out my hand to shake Kareem's hand. As we introduced ourselves the awesome pair stood up. I was literally dwarfed by their size.

"Nice to meet you." Kareem spoke first.

"I have great respect for your father. In fact, I don't usually come to these kind of events. I came today because of how important your dad was to me growing up." Bill Russell spoke earnestly as Kareem nodded his head in agreement. It reminded me once again of how much my father's life had meant to so many people, and what he had made possible.

As the reception wound down I took a seat next to my aunt Willa Mae and my uncle Mack, who had come in from Pasadena. A series of tributes preceded the introduction of my father. My parents were across from me. I watched Dad squeeze my mother's hand and, at one point, openly weep. When Dad rose to go to the podium, his gate was shaky and his voice cracked. I fought back the tears. I felt a warm glow as Dad introduced me as his secret love and praised Mom for being a powerful mother and loving wife. He made note that his mother, two sons, and Mr. Rickey were all missing and missed.

In his remarks my father talked about convictions, shared awards, and teamwork. To illustrate his point, he recalled a 1948 incident. According to Dad, members of Boston's Red Sox team tried to taunt Pee Wee Reese, a Southerner, for agreeing to play alongside him. He described how Reese left his position, came over to him, placed his hands on his shoulder, and said something. Dad couldn't remember his words. It didn't matter. Pee Wee's actions had great meaning.

I believe that the luncheon was particularly emotional for my father because with all the conflict with civil rights leaders he, too, needed to be reminded of his contributions. We had just gotten past this first celebration when Dad invited me to go with him to

hear Jesse Jackson speak at a Martin Luther King Jr. birthday celebration at the Apollo Theater. Understanding the importance of
group participation over the years, my father had remained hopeful that new leadership would emerge with a philosophy he could
live with. The opportunity had presented itself in the later part of
December when Jesse Jackson held a press conference to
announce the founding of People United to Save Humanity. My
father stood proudly at his side as a new celebrity recruit on the
seventy-five-member board. Dad found Jackson's economic vision
as appealing as his fiery, straightforward personality and youthful
spirit. The two men were drawn together at a crossroads in their
lives. To my father, Jesse Jackson represented hope for the future; to
Jesse, Dad was a link to the past.

After the announcement, Dad made frequent trips to Chicago
to lend his support as the grassroots organization took shape.
Whenever I saw Dad he was full of stories from his visits. The trips
to Chicago seemed to infuse vigor and possibility back into my
father. I was grateful to Jesse for that.

In January, my father invited me to go with him to the Apollo
Theater on 125th Street to hear Jesse Jackson speak in honor of
Dr. King's birthday. We arrived on the fifteenth, with an hour to
spare before the program was scheduled to begin. Dad settled me
in my seat before he went upstairs to hang out with "the fellas."
He loved to chat with Bobby Schiffman, whose family owned the
Apollo for years, and with his close friend, Peter Long, who
worked there. He was gone for about fifty minutes. By the time I
saw him making his way down the inner aisle, the auditorium was
nearly filled.

As Dad approached the third row, he stopped. He was squinting
right at me, just ten feet away from him. I watched, horrified. *My
father could not see me*. It took a few seconds for the shock to wear
off and for me to respond. I stood up and waved. Dad smiled and
began to make his way down the row toward me.

When Jesse Jackson asked my father to join him on stage, the
insides of my stomach jumped as I feared that Dad would trip and
fall trying to make it up the narrow steps. Dad was much too

proud to ask for help, but I was relieved to see an usher offer his hand as Dad began the ascent. He made it without tripping.

A month later, we saw Reverend Jackson again when my family was invited to Chicago by Operation PUSH. The plan was to honor Dad during the Saturday morning forum at the PUSH headquarters.

We flew into Chicago on two planes. I came in from Washington, D.C. Mom, Dad, and David arrived from New York on a plane not long after mine. On the Friday night of our arrival, there was a surprise showing of *The Jackie Robinson Story*. Reverend Jackson arrived to pick us up and escort our family to the theater. The auditorium was already darkened as we entered quietly, and the film played in its entirety to the cheers and applause of a packed auditorium. Unlike my reaction at the day camp, this time the film only spoke of triumph. As the credits began to roll and the audience was still applauding, Jesse Jackson walked to the front and proceeded to introduce each member of my family. As we came down, one by one, the audience cheered, whistling loudly. I had never experienced anything like that evening.

Saturday morning we were ushered into the PUSH headquarters and brought before the packed auditorium of once again cheering fans. Reverend Jackson presented my dad with a plaque and a medallion to mark the occasion. Before we left on Sunday, photographers came to my parents' suite to shoot a cover for *Sepia* magazine. Dad remarked that this was the last hurrah. As it turned out, the magazine was not released until after his death.

There had been so many tributes that year giving my family and me plenty of excuses to gather and celebrate. Once again they remain less significant in my memories than the frequent trips Dad made to Washington, D.C., on behalf of the Jackie Robinson Construction Company. He was meeting with representatives from the Department of Housing and Urban Development to negotiate for federally funded housing contracts. The frequency of the trips meant that Dad and I had lots of time to spend together.

When he was in Washington, we'd gauge our evening by how he

felt. Sometimes we'd go to a restaurant for dinner. At other times, Dad would be too tired and we would order room service and eat in his hotel room. I was content just being with him. We talked about everything from Freedom National Bank to my marriage.

"I'm thinking of going to medical school after I graduate from Howard," I said matter-of-factly. "I want to know more. What do you think?"

"I can remember the day when you weren't even sure if you could get through college. Now you're talking about medical school! I think it's great that you have come this far. You've gone from an insecure shy girl to a woman with confidence."

Pleased with his reaction, I continued. "Of course, I'll finish my nursing program first. Then, if I still feel this way I'll have to take some more science courses and you know how I hate chemistry! It would be a long haul before I even got to the point of applying to medical school." I seemed to be talking myself out of this plan before it got any further.

Dad, knowing me as he did, added, "Sharon, I don't care if you go to medical school or not. I'm just happy knowing that you have that much confidence to consider it. Come on, let's get out of here. I'm taking you shopping. You said that you needed a winter coat. Is there some place around here that we can find one?"

Shopping had always provided the bridge, an area of comfort, for us to be together. And, of course, I was always happy to provide Dad with the excuse. The year before my big need had been a car, so Dad and I went shopping one day and picked out a little red one. Dad had only one limitation to his generosity though: if possible, buy it wholesale. When I was a child, every Christmastime Dad would go to the garment district in Manhattan alone and return home with armloads full of men's clothing. It became quite a ritual. He would call my brothers and me into his room one by one to give us the opportunity to select a Christmas present for him from his latest stash. There would be golf shirts by the dozen, slacks, and socks. We would pick out what we wanted to give him and cart it off to our bedroom. Christmas morning the packages would be wrapped and placed under the tree. As Dad opened each one he would exclaim with joy that we had gotten him exactly what he wanted. It was such a silly game.

We left the restaurant and headed straight to the women's coat section of a nearby department store. The white saleslady steered me to the least expensive garments. I selected a red wool coat. I'd never worn red before. She took the coat and headed toward the cash register. On the way across the floor, I spotted a full-length, very stylish navy blue coat with a dramatic fur collar and fur cuffs. I stopped suddenly and stared at it.

"Looks like you've found one that you like better?" Dad asked.

"That coat is too expensive," the saleslady snapped.

I was already pulling it off the hanger and trying it on. I just had to see how it looked on me. The belt wrapped and wrapped then tied crisscross in the front. There was no doubt, the coat was stunning. I hugged it to me.

"We'll take it," Dad stated emphatically.

The saleslady's mouth fell open as she looked at my father in horror. Then she began to mumble what to me seemed like curse words under her breath. Dad gave her a stern, evil look. She didn't utter another word—not even a thank-you for our purchase. I still own that navy blue coat. I keep it stored in mothballs, waiting for one of my nieces to grow up to wear a size nine. Only then will I part with my coat.

Since we'd been together so much I figured that Dad wouldn't mind if I didn't accept his invitation to join my family in Cincinnati for the second game of the 1972 World Series during which he was to be honored. I was wrong. On a visit home the previous weekend, Mom, David, and I had threatened to boycott the event if Nixon was scheduled to appear. We did not want to give the appearance that we supported him, or his reelection bid. As it turned out we decided to suppress our political leanings for my dad's sake. I went back to school promising to call my father the following day. I had a legitimate excuse, we were in the midst of midterms. On the train ride back to school, I thought it over and as soon as I got home called Dad to tell him that I would meet them in Cincinnati. He was so pleased to get my call.

The next weekend I was on a flight that took less than two hours. I arrived in Cincinnati before my family, checked for their arrival gate, and hurried to meet them.

I spotted David first. Walking next to him was a woman I didn't recognize, but I was struck by her statuesque appearance. Must be Tish, David's new model girlfriend I'd heard about but hadn't met. It was strange seeing my bohemian brother's six-foot slender body clad in a gray suit and an obviously new pair of black dress shoes. David had seemingly traded his contempt for the trappings of the middle class and joined forces with the majority. Since his return from Africa, David had been driving Dad from our home in Stamford into Manhattan each day for work. This arrangement had stopped recently when David accepted a job writing for an independent film company based in Manhattan. My parents had hired a driver to take his place.

Dad's five-foot-eleven-inch, two-hundred-and-twenty-five-pound frame was stooped slightly. His long arms swung at his sides as he tried to maintain a steady gait. Mom and Dad were still a handsome couple though, and Mom looked stunning. Through sheer determination, she had maintained her size-ten figure and started wearing her mixed black and silver hair naturally. Her mocha chocolate complexion was flawless.

At breakfast the next morning David arrived in his gray suit once again. Dad teased David, with a mixture of joy and pride, about his one and only outfit. At each opportunity, Dad introduced Tish as David's fiancée. I now understand that my father was feeling the relief of living to see his youngest child become an adult.

As the World Series got under way the following afternoon, we laughed and cheered for both teams. The sun kept the October chill at bay. All day long people came by to greet Dad and he proudly introduced his family. Of all the stars on the field Dad was undeniably the hero, and it was clearly his day.

Although there had been many opportunities before for David and me to hear Dad tell the story of his early years in baseball, this was a day designed for memories. David, Tish, and I literally sat on the edge of our seats directly behind Mom and Dad asking question after question. I tried to envision the highly emotional and potentially volatile stands with their eyes on Number 42.

"Dad, if this was one of the segregated ballparks, where would the Jim Crow section be?" I asked. My eyes followed Dad's hand as he pointed toward the outfield section.

"The area would be so crowded that the fans would fill every square inch," Dad replied. "I never was quite sure if they didn't have enough seats or were just too excited to sit down," Dad added with a laugh. He told us how a cheer went up from the Jim Crow section at the smallest of his movements, like when he bent to tie his shoes.

"Weren't you too nervous to play?" David wanted to know.

"At times," Dad replied with a wistful look.

"Were you lonely?" I asked tentatively, fearful of his answer.

"Lonely . . . I had your mother in the stands and by my side each moment. That helped."

Dad fielded the questions with pride, not holding back the frustration at the lack of progress some twenty-five years later. He talked more of the mission than of the glory of the moment. He said he knew from the start that there was no quitting.

David and I absorbed every word silently, wishing that we had been there. I thought of some of the phrases used to describe Dad's finesse on the baseball diamond—the fire, the strategist, the multiple threat. People referred to his having been blessed with speed and coordination. They said that he seemed at his best when the pressure was the greatest and that the part of baseball he loved the most was running the bases.

Halfway through the game a representative from major league baseball came to get us. We had to walk a distance to get to the entrance to the field. The chatter stopped. An air of seriousness took over. Dad hadn't shared with us his remarks, but he gave the impression of a man on a mission.

As Dad was introduced a roar went up from the fans. I looked around but I couldn't see faces. Movement—yes. Voices—loudly. But expressions were lost. David, Tish, and I stood facing Mom and Dad. I fought back tears. Dad was squinting. I guess he, too, was trying to make out faces. Plaques were exchanged. A telegram was read from President Nixon, who apologized for not being able to attend the ceremonies. And to think we almost didn't come because we didn't want to appear to be supporting Nixon's reelection. I couldn't resist exchanging a smirk with David.

Finally, Dad took the microphone. It was hard to accept the fact that this man whom I loved so dearly was becoming more disabled each day. I watched him as he winced in pain, and stepped forward, barely able to see five feet in front of him.

Photographers, TV cameras, reporters, were everywhere. Millions of Americans were watching and listening. Dad made the appropriate introductions and thanked all those involved, cleared his throat, looked out into the stands, almost as if he could see those faces, and said: "When I look down the third base line, I want to see a black man coaching. Then I'll be able to say we've made progress."

That's all the press needed. Cameras flicked a mile a minute. The outspoken, controversial Jackie Robinson had done it again. On his day of glory, he had come to make a final statement to baseball and the world. He challenged them once again to take the leadership and integrate the ranks of management as they did the playing field some twenty-five years earlier. David and I exchanged smiles. We were especially proud of our father on this day.

Mom stood perfectly still, hands folded in front of her body, head held so high that it tilted slightly backward. Our mother was beside the man with whom she had shared so much. She was probably even more proud of him than David and I. Their marriage was a true partnership. At that moment, I don't believe Mom was concerned that her husband was resistant to her career. He was really the most important thing to her.

The jubilance of the day was beginning to fade. In its place was a somberness born out of the realities. Dad was right. Fundamentally, there were few changes. Certainly, there were more faces of color on the field, but that was all. Once the black athlete got too old to play professionally, the management side of sports offered him no opportunities. I had always thought my father would have been a great manager. I understood Dad's frustration with America.

After the game, we left the ballpark and the fans for a much deserved private time. It never ceased to amaze me how quickly Dad could step back into the role of father and husband. To the public, he was at his best on the baseball diamond. To me, it was when we had him all to ourselves. Over the years it had been our salvation as a family. Dad sensed that it was time to put the world aside and his turn to listen. Even that had changed over the last couple of years. I had changed, too. I had so much that I wanted to share.

That evening at dinner, Mom talked of her work at the Connecticut Mental Health Center and we listened. David described the film he was working on at the production company. Tish, her modeling aspirations. Dad filled us in on the construction company. And I held the family captive talking about my plans to do an independent study project with midwives in Jamaica, West Indies. We parted the next morning each to return to our full lives. I whispered to David that I liked Tish, gave them both a kiss, and hugged my parents for a long time, feeling an unusual sadness saying good-bye to my family.

17

A Temple of God

Two days after we returned from Cincinnati, Dad called me to say that he loved me.

"Hey, babe, did I wake you?" I sat straight up in bed and peered over at my alarm clock. Six forty-five, a little early, but after all, he had gotten up at six o'clock each morning for the last twenty years.

"Daddy!" A mixture of pleasure and fear raced through my mind. "Is everything all right?"

It was one of those perfectly clear autumn days. The sun reflected off the orange and yellow leaves on the maple tree that stood ten feet from the window of my efficiency apartment on Sixteenth Street. Joe lay next to me, dead to the world. He was still unemployed. I sighed as I looked down at his handsome face. The troubled state of our marriage was evidenced by the fact that I had gone to Cincinnati alone. I picked the phone up from the bedside table and walked to the other side of the room.

202   SHARON ROBINSON

"Yes, Sharon, everything is fine. I just wanted you to know how proud I was of you and David this past weekend. Thank you for making the extra effort to be there. It's not always easy for me to tell you how much I love you, but I hope you know that I do." Dad spoke softly into the phone.

Tears collected in my eyes. I took a deep breath before speaking. "I love you, too, Dad." My voice cracked in the middle of the sentence. My heart felt heavy. My family has never been the most expressive, so when someone actually said the words "I love you" out loud, it was time to take notice.

"I'll be in Washington on Thursday or Friday for meetings at HUD. You available for dinner?" Of course he knew I'd make myself available. We hung up, but I don't remember actually saying good-bye.

A few days after my father's call, I received another early morning call, this time from my mother. Her voice was unsteady. I froze . . . a massive heart attack . . . she was at the hospital. He was not expected to live . . . I mumbled something I assumed was intelligible but it didn't matter because Mom wasn't really listening. I put the phone back on its cradle, walked slowly to my closet, and began to put clothes into a bag. I told myself that I had to get home quickly. Mom needed me. I looked again at Joe. I should wake him and ask him to take me to the airport. The phone rang again. Joe stirred. I stared at the phone hesitantly. I didn't want to answer it. The ring . . . something about the ring.

"Hello," I heard myself say.

She was crying hysterically. Finally, I made out her words. "Your father's dead."

I felt like screaming but nothing came out—not even tears. "*Get home quickly . . . get home . . . quickly,*" played over and over in my head. I shook Joe.

"My father's had a heart attack. He's dead." I listened to the words. Maybe if I listened carefully, they wouldn't be true.

"Dead? I'm sorry, Sharon," Joe said. His hands shook. He hopped out of bed. We hugged. "I'm going with you." I knew that Joe genuinely loved and respected my father. Dad had accepted Joe from the beginning—and trusted him with his daughter, and he had been feeling like such a disappointment to him. Now he would never be able to make it up to Dad.

Taking slow, deliberate steps, we began to move about the apartment. Feeling at a complete loss, I welcomed Joe's direction, which he was capable of giving when the crisis was beyond his being. We had to pack. I had only one black dress. It was a fitted knit with large cables along the deep V neckline. Red and green stripes accented the sleeve. Thinking that I would wear it to the funeral, I grabbed the dress off its hanger. I considered whether to bring the four yards of African fabric that I used to wrap around my head for more formal occasions. I'd worn it for my wedding to Joe. I threw that material in my bag. I noticed Joe taking his dashikis off their hangers. I don't remember if Joe even owned a suit.

The world seemed so much slower. I was trying to hurry but my body would only move so fast. I glanced at the clock as we headed out of the apartment and noticed that it had only been an hour since Mom's call. Maybe the world will just stop, I thought.

Outside, men and women dressed in work clothes were standing at the bus stop. Students carrying books were piling out of my building and walking up the hill toward one of Howard's off-campus dormitories to catch the shuttle to school. The world was in motion as it was any other day. Didn't they know?

Joe found a cab to take us to National Airport. It took us to the Eastern Shuttle. Joe took our bags out of the trunk. I followed a few steps behind, trying to will myself the strength to keep up with him. Joe used our student IDs so that we could get discounted tickets. After our bags were safely on the conveyor belt, he grasped my hand, held it tightly, and guided me onto the plane.

I tried to keep up with the racing changes of pace that my mind took. I was afraid that if I started to cry I wouldn't be able to stop. If I had been home when he had his heart attack, I thought, could I have given him the mouth-to-mouth resuscitation we'd learned in medical-surgical nursing and possibly saved his life? Did he die instantly or suffer in pain? Did David make it from New York City in time to say good-bye?

Joe watched me closely, at one point pulling me into the shelter of his arms. I wept inside, so no tears showed. The stewardess offered us juice, coffee, or tea. I couldn't accept anything. The trip took forever. I needed to see Mom and David desperately, but I had to endure a taxi ride to the airport, a forty-five-minute plane ride, and then another hour taxi ride to our house in Stamford. Then I could cry.

Mom was in her bedroom. She had stopped crying but looked beaten down. It was a look I'd seen too often over the past couple of years, and with good reason, I thought. We hugged. "I'm okay," Mom said.

I went looking for my brother. He was in a hopeless state of constant motion, moving from one task to another. We were good soldiers. Taught early about survival, somehow we would endure. We'd had a dress rehearsal sixteen months ago. Both Jackie and Dad dead now. The core of the family. Just Mom, David, Grandma, and me now. I shuddered at the pressure David must feel.

Things would never be the same. I wondered what it would be like? I was also struck by the fact that I really didn't know how to communicate with my mother or brother. Since they were close, I also realized that I was the outsider. I was thankful for the flurry of activity that surrounded the house because it kept me from thinking too far ahead.

We began planning a final tribute, and the atmosphere was almost festive. I was completely entranced as I watched friends and relatives fill our house. Joe was loving and attentive, as he had been when Jackie died. I was thankful for his ability to come through in a crisis.

I took on the role of the woman of the house and played hostess. I must have given others the impression that I was handling my grief with strength and dignity. In fact, I was in an acute state of denial.

I was vaguely aware that there was a debate over who would be granted the honor of delivering my dad's eulogy. This was the only funeral detail to grab my attention. My mother, brother, and I wanted Jesse Jackson. There was some opposition voiced, but on this point we did not budge. In the end all agreed. Jesse Jackson would lead the program, which included the participation of a host of renowned national and local ministers.

I didn't want to go to Dad's wake. People kept telling me that I should go. I felt uneasy . . . pressured. I was defensive, even angry at times. I told family and friends that I wanted to remember my father as I had last seen him. No one bought my explanation.

When they returned from the viewing, they talked about "how peaceful he looked." I know they wanted me to feel better, but their words made me even more uncomfortable. I quietly excused myself from their discussions. I needed to spend time alone.

Later that evening, Dad's brothers Mack and Edgar arrived from Pasadena. I don't know what came over me. Possibly it was the absurdity of Uncle Edgar's outfit. He wore a checkered sport jacket, baggy trousers, and black high-top Converse sneakers. He seemed as vulnerable as I felt. Whatever the reason, the sight of Uncle Edgar sent me into hysteria. I fell into his arms, finally crying uncontrollably as I hadn't been able to do since Mom's phone call. I clung to Uncle Edgar as he swayed back and forth, repeating, "There, there, child." Uncle Edgar, as uncomfortable as I must have made him feel, did not stop patting my back or release me until I had regained my composure.

The morning of the funeral was sunny with a deep chill. I was so nervous that I worried about crazy things like, "Would my contact lenses float away if I cried?" Since I had difficulty seeing more than ten feet in front of me I had a serious dilemma. I must have stood for a good ten minutes silently debating the merits of glasses versus contact lenses. I was deliberating silently when a family member came into my mother's bathroom and handed me a Valium. By the time the limousine arrived to take us on our dreaded journey, I was calm.

I climbed into the backseat of the limousine next to my husband. My mother and brother sat across from Joe and me. I rested my head against the side of the car and closed my eyes. In silence we were driven from our home in Stamford to 122nd Street and Riverside Drive in New York City. As the limousine pulled up in front of Riverside Church, I looked out at the faces in the crowd and realized that I could no longer postpone the inevitable. It was obvious by the sadness on their faces that these people were not here to celebrate Dad's accomplishments. They were here to say good-bye. I found myself being guided out of the limousine, passively accepting my fate and allowing myself to be led up the stone steps and into the small chapel.

I forced my eyes to the front of the chapel, where an elaborate gray and blue metallic casket sat. I was relieved to see that it was closed.

The peace was abruptly disturbed by Uncle Mack's arrival. He was insisting that the casket be opened so that the family could have a final viewing. I jumped out of my seat in protest almost shouting, "You promised no open casket!" My greatest fear was about to become reality. I did not want to see my father's stiff body. Joe held me tightly against him.

The casket was opened briefly before the service began. Reverend Jackson and Reverend Wyatt Tee Walker, activist and pastor of Cannon Baptist Church, led family members to it for a final good-bye. David held Mom up. I didn't move. The casket, draped in red roses, was closed for the last time.

Music from the main chapel signaled the beginning of the services. Reverend Earnest Campbell escorted Mom as the congregation stood and turned toward the procession. We sat in the front row.

I looked around at the packed chapel. Those who were unable to get seats stood along the two outer aisles and in the hallway. Thousands gathered outside and listened to the service on loudspeakers. Everybody who was somebody was there, from Dad's baseball teammates to other baseball stars and even presidents of teams. I remember seeing Joe Louis, Dick Gregory, Hank Aaron, Vida Blue, Elston Howard, and Willie Mays. A. Philip Randolph, the labor union executive, sat tall and imposing, while Roy Wilkins, executive director of the National Association for the Advancement of Colored People, looked unusually somber. Bowie Kuhn, commissioner of baseball, rubbed his eyes. And President

Nixon sent a forty-man delegation led by White House counselor Robert Finch.

Then a soloist stepped to the podium to sing, "Nobody Knows the Trouble I've Seen." Our longtime friend Reverend Lacy Covington read scriptures, which preceded a spiritual message from Reverend Wyatt Tee Walker. Grandma's minister, Reverend George Lawrence, read a prayer and the Recording Choir of Canaan Baptist Church led right into the eulogy.

I sat very still, feeling numb, with a pocket full of tissues.

Finally, Reverend Jesse L. Jackson came forward. "His body was a temple. A temple which was used to achieve God's will. When Jackie took the field in 1947, something reminded us of our birthright to be free. For he'd demonstrated to us that something could be done. His body was a temple of God, but his mind found no peace in wickedness. His powerful arms lifted not only bats but barriers. So, let us mix the bitter with the sweet. He created ripples of possibility which seven years later the Supreme Court decision confirmed."

As he spoke so eloquently about what my father's life had meant to a people, a nation, a world, I found myself losing the battle to deny the magnitude of my loss.

"In this last dash Jackie has stolen home. His body will rest but his spirit, mind and his impact are perpetual and affixed to human progress as are the stars in heaven. No grave can hold this body down. It belongs to the ages."

As Reverend Jackson's tone lowered, Roberta Flack's voice could be heard growing louder in the background as she began, "I Told Jesus."

The casket was carried out of the church by Bill Russell, Don Newcombe, Jim Gilliam, Ralph Branca, Pee Wee Reese, and Joe Black. Governor Rockefeller, whose family had financed the construction of the stone church, was an honorary pallbearer. I felt a flood of relief as the service ended.

The mile-long motorcade traveled a carefully planned route through Harlem and ended just a few blocks from the site of the old Ebbets Field at Cypress Hills Cemetery in Brooklyn.

Thousands of mourners lined the streets as if providing a protective shield. People hung out of their windows, others waved from
rooftops. Children tried to touch the hearse. People cheered
"Good-bye Jackie, good-bye." Adults openly mourned the passing
of a friend and symbol to the community.

I was only marginally aware of what was happening outside. I
looked out of the tinted window as the limo came to an abrupt
halt. We were in front of Freedom National Bank and the Apollo
Theater. A few people peered into our car window, but mostly
they respected our grief and displayed their own. Dad would have
liked this, I thought.

We continued east on 125th Street, over the Triboro Bridge and
on to Brooklyn. I settled into Joe's arms. We were all silent. Finally,
this last leg of the journey ended. The limo pulled up next to the
curve on a hill. The trees were shades of gold and red. The grass
was still green. It was a peaceful setting. I knew that my father was
to be buried in the grave alongside my brother. I felt strangely
happy about this arrangement. At least they were together.

EPILOGUE

It took me years to fully accept my father's death, but not long to integrate myself into my reconstituted family. We were too needy to be independent. So Mom, David, and I clung to each other for strength, forming a bond and support for each other that got us through those early years.

Rebirth became a theme for Mom, David, and me. We each had to find our way in our newly defined world. Mom had a choice when Dad died. She could remain at Yale University or enter the business world. Choosing the latter, she stepped forward as president of the Jackie Robinson Construction Company and founder and chairman of the newly formed Jackie Robinson Foundation. David and I are active board members of the Jackie Robinson Foundation but it is Mom's baby. Under her leadership it grew from a small local foundation to a national institution which supports a minimum of thirty new four-year scholars each year and boasts a graduation rate of ninety-two percent.

In the beginning, Mom found living in our Stamford house too painful without Dad. She closed it up and moved into a co-op apartment in Manhattan. When the two-bedroom duplex adjacent to Mom's apartment came on the market, David bought it. Six months later, when I graduated from Howard University, I formally separated from Joe, accepted a nursing job in New York City, and moved solo into a brownstone a block over from Mom and David and in the same house as Candy. Even with the security of being surrounded by my family and closest friend, that first year was difficult, especially when my grandmother died in June.

As we healed, Mom, David, and I felt comfortable with some distance. Mom moved back to our house in Stamford and commuted each day into the city to assume the role of president of the Jackie Robinson Construction Company. David sold his co-op, married Joyce Ware Thomas, and moved into Harlem. And I moved to Los Angeles. For years, I lived a bicoastal life and considered myself a free spirit, only taking casual notice of my propensity to avoid attachment. It took me years to acknowledge that one result of the profound losses was a fear of intimacy. This is a challenge I struggle with on a daily basis.

Professionally, my life has proceeded smoothly and with great satisfaction. At twenty-six, I graduated from Columbia University's School of Nursing with a master's degree in maternity nursing, passed the nurse-midwifery certifying exam, and joined the modern version of an ancient order. Fascinated with birth from childhood, raised by my mother to nurture, fueled by observing my parents find fulfillment in a life of service, I accepted my calling when it came. It was a long curvy road. For a while I carefully kept my statistics. Fifty births within the first six months of practice . . . one hundred within a year . . . two hundred and fifty after five years. Lovingly my hands ushered new life into this world.

My mother has entered her seventh decade with the same beauty, grace, and vitality that she exuded in her twenties. I study my mother as she plans to age with the same finesse that she lived her life. I am proud of my mother's accomplishments. Mom talks now of succession and I step up to the plate ready. I am learning

to assume some of the family responsibility without compromis-
ing what is most important to me, my home.

Over the years, my brothers and I have produced and adopted a
total of nine children and one great-grandchild. Rachel, a relaxed,
loving grandmother, lavishes this next generation with love, care,
and attention and encourages them to live up to her high standards
of excellence.

Sonya Pankey, Jackie's only child, has grown into a beautiful
woman and loving parent. She lives in New York City with her
daughter, Sherita.

David, the father of seven, has learned to balance his work with
his family. He has two adopted children and five biological daughters. When David and Joyce divorced ten years ago, he moved to
Tanzania, East Africa, where he later married a delightful, loving
woman, Ruti. David and Ruti own a house on the beach in
Mjimwema and a 120-acre coffee farm in the Mbozi District. Six
of his seven children also live in Tanzania. I applaud my brother's
vision and determination but also find it ironic that he, a child of
privilege, has flourished in a country where electricity is a luxury,
transportation a major challenge, and education available to the
minority. To me, his decision is as much testament to the alienation
African-American males often feel within their own country as it
is a commitment to internationalism.

The lessons of my life have taught me to live each day to its
fullest without regrets or anger. Work is important but what brings
me the most joy is my home. This became clearest to me in 1976
when I met and fell in love with Robert Simms, and together we
produced a son, Jesse Martin Robinson Simms. While our union
did not survive, raising my son as a single parent has brought fullness and meaning into my life. I have lovingly guided my son's
growth, the development of his values, and tried to prepare him for
adulthood.

I often wonder how my father would feel about the lives
David and I have chosen for ourselves. It is clear that we have
internalized the Robinson legacy of service and commitment to
our people. I am certain that Dad would be pleased with our

productiveness, but he, like Mom, would be worried by the unconventional routes we have taken. Dad would admire David's commitment, fortitude, and courage but would not have liked the fact that his son chose to live outside the United States. He would have been concerned about us raising our children as single parents and been relieved when we remarried. My father would have been intrigued but not surprised by my decision to become a midwife. He would have found my stories of traveling the beach community outside Los Angeles on a bicycle with a beeper strapped to my jean shorts a bit eccentric. And, like my son, he wouldn't have wanted to know the specifics about deliveries. Only my mother takes delight in the details.

Dad, like Mom, would have relaxed during my years of teaching at such prestigious universities as Columbia, Howard, and Yale. Teaching is easy for everyone to understand. The modern version of midwifery is harder to grasp.

He would have accepted my decision in 1989 to leave midwifery temporarily to work with Jesse Jackson as executive director of PUSH for Excellence. Dad would have been amused by my first introduction to a PUSH audience when the minister who presented me added with pride that I had gone from delivering babies to delivering a nation of children. I remember wondering if that was possible. And, most likely, my father would have appreciated my decision to return, after eight years of working for the nonprofit world, to my first love: teaching and practicing midwifery.

I am amazed at both the similarities and differences in my son's and my childhood. It goes beyond the obvious. Hoping to give my son a solid foundation to balance out the fact that he would not grow up with the daily presence of his father, I surrounded him with productive black people. We lived in black neighborhoods, his pediatrician was black as was his dentist. But education required a compromise. He has been educated in private schools because he needed the small structured environment that they offered. Yet, in each of his schools, children of color were outnumbered but representative.

I have marveled at my son's vision, clear direction, and sensitivity toward others. At five, Jesse described to me the banking institution he planned to own one day. At twelve, he talked of combining law and business like his father. Now seventeen, Jesse stands over six foot three and has concentrated his considerable athletic prowess on football, which he plans to pursue at least through college.

I regret that my father will never know his grandchildren nor they him. From the oldest, Sonya, to the babies yet to be born, they have come to know the man and his accomplishments only through the colorful images and memories of others.

As my father stole home for the final time, October 24, 1972, I prayed that my wailings would turn to dancing. My prayers have been answered. With the passage of time, I learned to focus on the life we shared with Dad and Jackie rather than dwell on the pain of the loss. In the process, I've noticed that life hasn't necessarily gotten any easier; we just deal with it better. In 1997, we will celebrate the fiftieth anniversary of my father's entry into baseball. While my family will join the country in celebrating this stellar aspect of Dad's life, we will also celebrate the loving father and husband that he was, and the proud family tradition of service that resulted from his example.